*"Everything has its wonders, even darkness and silence, and I learn whatever state I may be in, therein to be content."*–Helen Keller

To my mom, Sally Schiller.
With her sight, she has given me eyes to see.
With her breath, she has given me wings to fly.

# Messenger
*between*
# Worlds

# About the Author

Kristy Robinett is a world-renowned revolutionary psychic medium and author of *Ghosts of Southeast Michigan: Michigan's Haunting Legends and Lore* and the *Higher Intuitions Oracle* deck. She specializes in bringing humor to what most people fear and inspires all ages to ignite the light within them so that the fire of inspiration continues on. It's Kristy's down-to-earth style, honesty, sense of humor, and warmth that makes her a sought-out coach and speaker.

Kristy has been profiled on many radio programs, including *Coast to Coast AM*, and several television shows. She's read for a blushing clientele of who's who in Hollywood along with law enforcement, clergy, politicians, physicians, attorneys, domestic goddesses, local celebrities, and everybody else in between.

Kristy is a wife and mom to four children and many animals. She loves glitter, fuzzy socks, ice cream, and hugs. Visit www.tangledwishes.com to view upcoming events or to contact Kristy for a session.

Linda —
Always Know you are
guided!

# Messenger *between* Worlds

True Stories from a Psychic Medium

## Kristy Robinett

Llewellyn Publications
Woodbury, Minnesota

FIRST EDITION
First Printing, 2013

Book design by Bob Gaul
Cover art © Maarigard/Bigstock.com
Cover design by Adrienne Zimiga
Editing by Ed Day

Llewellyn Publications is a registered trademark of Llewellyn Worldwide Ltd.

**Library of Congress Cataloging-in-Publication Data**
Robinett, Kristy.
  Messenger between worlds: true stories from a psychic medium/Kristy Robinett.—
First Edition.
    pages cm
  ISBN 978-0-7387-3666-2
1. Mediums—United States—Biography. I. Title.
  BF1283.R657A3 2013
  133.9'1—dc23
                                        2012051685

Llewellyn Publications
A Division of Llewellyn Worldwide Ltd.
2143 Wooddale Drive
Woodbury, MN 55125-2989
www.llewellyn.com

Printed in the United States of America

*Although this is a work of nonfiction, some names, characters, places, and incidents have been changed.*

# Contents

# Acknowledgments

The support that I have received from friends and fans has been overwhelming. Without the constant urging to write a book, this work would probably still be sitting in a dusty file beneath photo albums and other memories. So, I first thank all of you who have pestered me through the years to publish this book.

I want to thank my husband, Chuck Robinett. With friendship, respect, and love, he has walked beside me through a very interesting and sometimes challenging journey, and I am eternally grateful.

Thank you to my children, Micaela and Connor, for their strength and constant love.

Thank you also to my stepdaughters, Cora and Molly, for their acceptance and their love.

Thank you to Kerry Combs for believing in me and befriending me during your difficult time. I also want to thank the following individuals, without whose contributions and support this book would not have been written: Donna Shorkey, Jenni Licata, Mary Byberg, and Laura Bohlman.

# Introduction

My mom taught me at a young age to be myself no matter what. Although she was my cheerleader, I didn't have a strong role model because, ironically, she hadn't followed her own advice. It would take me more than thirty years to feel comfortable with who I was and the gifts that I was born with. And then there are always lessons to be learned, life tests to be taken, and judgment to dodge.

Writing this book brought up many painful memories that were buried in my subconscious mind, and yet I found as I listened to my soul's whispers that I also had begun to heal. The bandages I used to mask myself were becoming weighty and dingy and were starting to unravel, so it was best to remove them rather than put on fresh wrappings to continue disguising my tattered soul.

We all have skeletons in the closet, and, while not all of them need to be dug up and made to perform, many of them need to be given a proper burial. *Messenger Between Worlds* is an account of my own very talented chorus line.

As you may know, I am a psychic medium. It was difficult ignoring what I once referred to as "my personal curse." When a ghost is adamant about discussing his/her passing and begging for help, it's a bit like having a pink polka-dotted elephant tap dancing in your living room. You either try to ignore it while everything around you is destroyed, or you learn to embrace it. I have *finally* done the latter.

Your personal curse doesn't have to be the secret of seeing the dead. I claim that as my own! It could be that you want to be a gymnastics teacher instead of an accountant, aspire to be a writer instead of a barista, or dream of having a nurturing relationship instead an abusive one. Maybe you just want to feel rewarded by life. Becoming comfortable with my gift, with myself, has taken an awfully long time, and still when I speak with someone who doesn't know *what* I am, I begin: "Now, I'm perfectly sane, but... I see ghosts." I'm not different from you. Everybody—you, included—has the ability to *see*; you just have to open yourself to it. I hope to give you the same self-acceptance and the ability to *see* through your own situations so that you can find your way back on the path of life fulfillment.

Growing up I didn't go around saying I wanted to be a professional psychic medium. Instead I dreamt of being a prosecuting attorney. It began with my love of true crime novels and anything involving Nancy Drew. I read every single book in order to figure out whodunit. It's funny how, even though I don't have the law degree, I *still* find myself helping with the whodunit!

Since I was the age of three, spirits have come to me in the dead of night, telling me of their woes. Some stand. Some sit. All have their own story to share. It could be that they have been murdered, are frightened to cross over, or have a message to get to a family member. My nighttimes have always been annoying, to say the least. The continuous line of spirits who stand, single file, next to my bed is reminiscent of the DMV on a Monday morning. If I could only figure out how to affix a "Take a Number" machine to my energy, I'd be all set. It wasn't until I grew older that I realized I was a counselor to the dead at night and a counselor to the living by day whether I liked it or not. Straddling both worlds is exhausting and exhilarating.

"Does this happen often?" I evenly asked the middle-aged lady sitting across from me as I ducked the second cobalt blue teacup that sailed past my head. I watched as it fell to the ground without breaking.

"It started a few weeks ago. He seems to like dishes the best," Celia responded. "I've asked him to throw something softer, but he seems to like dishes the best," she repeated, ducking a matching plate.

Her house was a typical 1970s ranch with a family inside to match. I had received the call from Celia asking if I would do a paranormal investigation and a house blessing. She stated that odd things were happening.

Odd didn't quite describe it.

The air in the three-bedroom house was heavy with negative emotion and fear. Part of the fear was, no doubt, coming from me. Even after what feels like umpteen years of doing investigations, I am still in awe at times and still get scared. My husband sat next to me with one eyebrow raised ever so slightly as he looked at the unexplainable chaos. He silently shook his head and gave me a sideways smirk. He married into the crazy life of a psychic medium and has always said he just "came along for the beer," although neither of us drink anything harder than Diet Pepsi. I don't need spirits to see spirits.

I was born with "the gift," but growing up, it seemed to cause more trouble than it was worth. My father was extremely religious—a well-respected deacon of the Missouri Synod Lutheran church. I was taught from early on that anything ghostly or psychic was of the devil. So, when I saw spirits at the age of three and communicated with them, explaining it wasn't exactly the kind of heart-to-heart talk I wanted to have with my parents. To be honest, that chat with Dad *still* hasn't happened. I confess, I'm not great with confrontation. I kept the gift hidden—sort of. I loved making predictions and sharing them with my friends, especially if I *knew* there was going to be a pop quiz or that a particular couple was going to break up or get together. When asked how I knew about these things before they happened, I made up lame excuses like it was a lucky guess or I had a feeling. The toughest part of the gift comes with situations like plane crashes or other disasters, and they still have quite an impact on me. When September 11th happened and I had a vision a few days beforehand, I blamed myself for not doing anything other than scribbling some drawings, names, dates, and other miscellaneous things in my journal. If I wasn't given this gift to help, then why was I given it at all? It's still a question I often ask myself.

So, what is a psychic medium? For some, images of flowing gowns, smoldering incense, and airy-sounding women come to mind. Ha! That is so not me. Flowing gowns? I tend to gravitate toward jeans and cute T-shirts. Incense? I just don't like the smell, but I do burn white sage! And the airy voice? Hmm...my husband may call me an airhead sometimes, but he says it in a loving way! In a nutshell, as a psychic medium, I talk to those who have crossed over to what is sometimes called heaven or the Other Side, along with spirit guides, and I pass along information they give me. It's different from a psychic, who uses earthly tools (tarot, pendulum, etc.) to foretell the future. Readings with me are never of the cookie-cutter variety. I have a sense of humor, and I like to use it in the readings. I still remember the first time I went for a reading for myself. I was incredibly nervous, convinced that the medium would tell me all bad and nothing good. Instead, I was immediately put at ease by his friendliness and lack of skinned black cats. I felt like I was talking to a friend. That's how I want my readings to be, and I strive to achieve that with everybody I read. I do, however, take my police work very seriously. Missing persons and murder cases are tough, especially when they deal with children. I've had my share of tears working on cases with police and private investigators. And paranormal investigations, although they can be fun, they can also be stressful and dangerous. It isn't always the ghosts or demons you have to fear, but the living. I've had death threats from angry cheating husbands, and I've been stalked by killers who thought I knew too much. There's never a dull moment in my life and for that I am thankful, as I am easily bored. Sometimes I wait to hear "Cut!" from a director and have it all shut off, but my life is real. Sometimes surreal, sure, but still real.

I love being a psychic medium. I love doing readings, radio, and television. I used to hide, but I'm no longer an undercover psychic medium, just a psychic medium. I will scream it from the rooftop.

Okay, maybe not. I'm afraid of heights.

Meanwhile, let's get back to poor Celia. Remember her? She's the client we left in the line of cups-and-saucer fire in that three-bedroom ranch house. As it turned out, Celia's problem was an older gentleman (in spirit form) who had once lived in the house. He was very upset that the family was renovating the kitchen. I had a talk with this stubborn spirit-in-residence, and we made a deal: he'd stop pitching china at Celia if she'd keep the dishes in the same spot that his wife had always kept them—next to the stove instead of next to the sink. Another mystery solved and problem re-solved. If only they were all that easy!

I am the messenger between worlds.

# one

# Kids See the Darnedest Things

I received my first spanking when I was three years old. That might not be unusual, except for the circumstances. Instead of being brought on by a childish temper tantrum, the punishment was for talking to the so-called dead and predicting death.

My maternal grandmother was coming to visit, and I was entertaining a house full of spirits. My family couldn't see the spirits, so they disregarded my constant communication with what they labeled "imaginary friends." They considered me an overly imaginative and creative child, but they didn't know what was really going on. Or did they? I frustrated my parents to no end with the constant chatter and, on this particular day, things came to a head.

Just minutes before my mom's parents, Helen and Grant, arrived, an older spirit appeared, claiming to be my great-grandmother, Helen's mother. She told me that the angels were coming soon for Grandma Helen, who in retrospect was often quite sickly, but nobody expected her to pass away. The spirit told me that I needed to say my goodbyes and to prepare my mom by letting her know the same. When my grandma came, I shared the information with her and my mom, and refused to let her sit down because the angels were coming. Looking back on this, I'm sure I frightened both of them with the death warning. It wasn't that I was a malicious child—in fact, I was quiet and shy—but I felt I was doing exactly what I had been asked to do. My mom grew so frustrated with me that she swatted me on my rear.

I knew that I was different from the beginning of my memory. Spirits would move around me during nighttime. Some of them talked to me, while others were just happy that I could see them, and yet others loved to tease and frighten me. I didn't know that nobody else saw them until I could speak and point them out.

"Oh look, Kristy has invisible friends!" the family would proclaim in a mocking way. But they weren't invisible to me—they were as real as my own family standing in front of me was. I couldn't quite comprehend how and why I was seeing them, and yet, they weren't.

Six months later, Grandma Helen *unexpectedly* passed away and my first prediction came to light.

"How did you know grandma was going to die?" my mom asked me the morning before the funeral.

"Each time I saw her, I saw more and more angel feathers around her," I answered. "And the lady with the worn hands told me."

My mom gave me a strange look. "I see death too, Kristy, but I see crows."

I was too young to understand what she meant. I should have felt as if I had an ally, but instead I felt confused. One minute my mom was punishing me, and the next she was curious.

The evening before Grandma Helen's burial, I sat on the green shag carpet with my pale white legs crossed Indian style, making me look tinier than I already was. I watched as my mom pieced together a sewing project. When my mom was sad, she would either withdraw or sleep for days, or she would keep herself incredibly busy so that she couldn't think about anything other than the task at hand.

"Why Kristy?" I pondered out loud, ever curious, but more than that, I needed answers.

"Why Kristy, what?" she responded, perplexed and a bit short.

"I don't understand why you named me Kristy when my name is Sara. And that is Sara without an 'h', but everybody always spelled it with an 'h'!"

"You don't like your name?" My mom gave me a strange look. She grabbed a cigarette with her long, lean fingers, lit it, and took a long drag. "You're named after my favorite book,

*Christy* by Catherine Marshall. Sara was never even on our name list."

I started to tear up, confused how to further explain. "But I know that my name is Sara and not Kristy."

I had an affinity for old-fashioned names. My favorite stuffed dolls and stuffed animals were named Hannah, Mary, Anna, Ezekial, Abigail, etc. There was never a Jennifer or Michael in the bunch. And, the more stuffed animals and stuffed dolls that surrounded me, the more secure I felt, almost as if they were the large family that I didn't have and yearned for.

The Sara name debate continued for years. I never asked anybody to call me Sara, but I just knew that I wasn't a Kristy. Both my mom and my dad informed me that if I still felt the same way when I turned sixteen, they would allow me to change my name, but by that time I was certain my friends would think I was crazy. Honestly, how do you go sixteen years as one name, only to suddenly change it to another? You don't. And I didn't. Many people have asked me why I don't use Sara as a pseudonym or stage type of a name, and the reason I don't is that it is much more special than just a fake name—it was and always will be my soul's name.

I wasn't allowed to go to the funeral, but I can still remember sitting in my bedroom with my Fisher Price castle, quietly humming and playing when I saw a bright white shadow in the doorway. I raised my hand to my eyes to shield the brilliance of the light. I had nowhere to run except through the light, so I just sat and stared. It was only a few seconds when I heard a familiar voice.

"Take care of your mommy, Kristy, and tell her that I love her, but I am happy here."

I knew then that it was Grandma Helen. But I already had gotten a spanking for predicting her death; wouldn't I get the same for bringing a message afterwards? I thought I would, so I just stayed quiet.

Even though Grandma Helen had passed on and left her husband and her daughter, my uncles had passed away just a few years beforehand and everybody missed them. I could only imagine the reunion she had with her sons as they met her on the Other Side.

So with my mom's sadness for her mother's loss, the talk of my name not being my name, and the constant conversations with so-called invisible friends, my mom thought that perhaps I was bored or lonely and marched my four-year-old self up to the local Lutheran school for an admissions test. The school informed my parents that I was mature enough to start school and I was granted an early entrance.

School was something I was good at, but didn't much like. I didn't fit in with the kids and related much better with the adults. And, although I had strong opinions, I was painfully shy. Kindergarten, a time that's supposed to be filled with the happiness of playing and coloring, was, instead, just plain awful.

My teacher was a large woman with a booming voice, not the sweet, grandmotherly type that you would visualize teaching kindergarten. In fact, she reminded me a lot of my dad's mother. It was a common occurrence for me to be sent to the corner many times for senseless things—well, at least I thought they were senseless.

Every morning the teacher would tell a Bible story and then ask the class questions about the story. One morning I was called on to answer the question, but I had been preoccupied by the teacher's father, who was in spirit, and who wouldn't leave me alone. "You have to tell her that she has diabetes," he kept saying, nudging me. The message was just too large for a child to understand and too complicated to explain to anybody, and so I shook my head at him. My teacher thought I was being sassy in not replying to her question. Truth be told, I didn't know the answer; I was much too busy trying to shrug off her concerned father. A ruler was smacked on the desk and I was sent into the corner until I could answer the question, which resulted in a whole morning of sitting in that same corner making friends with a spider (which I still remember naming Dosey) and being very angry at my teacher's father. My mom picked me up at school and on the walk home I vented, obviously removing the part of talking to a dead man and complaining instead about being sent to the corner. "If I didn't know the answer to the question when the teacher asked it the first time, how would I know it later on?" I asked her. My reasoning often resulted in an amused grin from my mom.

The spirit of my teacher's father bothered me that entire year with various messages that I knew I couldn't share for fear of being disciplined. For fear of not being believed. For fear.

"Tell her I'm sorry," he said. "Please ... you can see me. Tell her." I just shook my head and tried to avoid him as much as I could.

That year couldn't have gotten over fast enough. But if I thought kindergarten was bad, first grade was even worse.

# two

# Guided

When my Native American guide presented himself at the end of my bed when I was three years old, to say that I was startled would be putting it mildly. I'm pretty sure that I screamed and ran down the stairs as fast I could. Standing over six feet tall, with dark skin and a scowl on his face, he wasn't exactly who you would expect to be a child's spirit guide. But he was *my* guide, and he took his job extremely seriously. It wasn't until he came in a dream where he explained that he was my protector, forever and ever, that I understood that he meant no harm.

Alto, a man, or spirit, of few words, brings me my night visions, and he helps me believe in my daytime dreams. At such a young age, I was completely unaware of his role in my life, and since I was repeatedly told that ghosts and spirits do not exist, I was confused as to why I could see him. I could touch him, and I could hear him, just as well as I could my own parents and my siblings. He was no different to me than any person who walked this earth—except that nobody else could see, hear, or touch him. He didn't float like people envision ghosts. He wasn't transparent. He wore clothes, he had expressions, and he spoke in full sentences. At that early age, he would tell me stories of the places he had lived and of his family in North Carolina. He would also tell me one day that I would write and tell my own stories. It was a lot of information to take in as a kid.

A year later, I noticed another spirit that was around Alto. The house was sometimes so full of spirits that it was difficult to decipher who was a guide or who was just a spirit hitchhiker. This spirit had long strawberry blonde hair, with a slight wave. Her skin was the color of peaches, and her demeanor much less intense than Alto's personality. She was soft-spoken, mild-mannered, and, most of all, patient with both me and Alto.

One day as my parents were arguing, I closed my eyes to wish myself away, and when I opened them, the Irish beauty stood in front of me. Her gentle turquoise eyes were enough to reassure me that everything was all right. "I'm Tallie," she said. But instead of hearing her as if she was in the room with me, her voice resonated in my head telepathically. Her voice held a slight Irish accent that was calming. It startled me for a moment before she explained that it was easier for her to communicate that way. It would also make it easier in a crowd. I wouldn't have to look for her like I did for Alto. Instead, I would first feel her energy around me—an energy that felt like warm towels out of the dryer and a scent that smelled like clean linens— and then she would talk to me. She also made sure not to startle me, unlike Alto, who I think thought it was funny. (Although he rarely smiled, I could see the smile within him.) I was like his daughter, and for Tallie, I was like her favorite niece. My love for them grew as our relationship developed. Through dreams, journaling in my diary, and daydreaming, I was able to build the communication and figure out the personalities and their roles in my life—and mine in theirs. They became an instrumental part of my life and my growth, yet it would be several decades before I recognized the true importance of our relationship, and the importance of spirit guides in the lives of others.

At the same time I started to recognize my guides, my household was falling apart. My mom's mother had crossed over, my mom was going through an array of undiagnosed ailments, and my older siblings were entering their teenage years, which generated the usual trials and tribulations for our parents.

One warm afternoon my mom and dad were once again having another argument. Well, my mom was having an argument while my dad stayed silent, ignoring her, which only infuriated her more. Mom screamed, yelled, and threw things, doing everything and anything to get his attention, but he stayed stoic, staring at the television.

"Fine," she said, "I'm just going to kill myself."

I did what I always did when they fought; I held on to my stuffed animals and cried.

She looked over at me, her blue eyes blazing with anger. "Are you coming, or do you want to be stuck with *him?*"

Even though I was only a child, I knew the depth of every single word she said. She wanted to die, and she wanted me to die with her. I didn't want to die. I didn't want to kill myself. I sat motionless on the stairwell that could easily take me to my bedroom where I could hide underneath my blankets. Instead of running, I mentally begged my father to do something, to say something, and stop the ridiculous argument. But he continued to sit in his chair and stare at the television screen.

"Fine," she repeated, and stormed out the front doorway.

I ran over to the screened door to see her walk off the porch and turn left down the street.

"Do something," I begged out loud at my father, but sensing that he wasn't going to do anything, I ran after her myself.

"I love you, Mommy," I told her over and over as we continued walking.

She pulled out a cigarette and lit it with her shaky hands. Tears uncontrollably poured down her face.

About a half mile away was a small bridge that overlooked a river. "I should just jump," she said. "*We* should just jump."

I was heaving now, physically ill. I didn't want to die. I didn't want my mom to die. And I loved my father. I threw up on the sidewalk, and continued to beg my mom to stop and walk back home. "You won't go to heaven, Mommy," I told her in between heaves. "You won't see grandma or Uncle Freeman or Uncle Mel. You won't!"

At the mention of heaven, I felt a presence around me, a warmth as if someone was hugging me, and saw Alto and Tallie standing next to me with a crowd of spirits, some of which had wings. Angels.

"It will be all right," I heard Alto say telepathically.

As if my mom also sensed the peaceful presences, her tears stopped. She grabbed my hand and, without a word, led me back to the house.

By the time we got home, my father's mother, Francis Schiller, was there. Instead of feeling as if everything was all right, I screamed to Alto out loud, "How is this okay? Please just make this okay!" I begged.

But nobody was paying attention to me. Instead, my grandmother was screaming at my mother.

"You're sick, Sally. You are sick!"

My grandmother was a heavy woman with a loud voice who despised me from the moment of my conception. When my mom announced her pregnancy with me, my grandmother told her that she would drive her to get an abortion and instructed my mom to get in the car. My grandmother's attitude toward me didn't get much better after I was born. My brother was eleven years older than I was and my sister was nine years older, so I suppose she figured that just as my mom and dad could finally begin having a life, I came and broke up that party.

I constantly asked both my mom and dad why grandma didn't like me and they would only shake their head as if they didn't know why, or at least how to explain it.

The strangeness of my gift just added another issue to the already heated hate, and predicting my other grandma's passing just a couple years before, I kept thinking that maybe she was just afraid of me. Maybe she thought I made my grandma die and would do the same thing to her. I think my grandmother tried to like me; she even told my dad that we needed to go to counseling in order to help heal our relationship, but my dad, who never liked confrontation, laughed at his mother and asked her how much healing could be done—I was just a child!

Grandma Schiller had become pregnant with my father at the age of thirteen and claimed to be raped. Her parents had objected to getting rid of the baby. Motherly instincts had a difficult time settling in, and the lie regarding the rape became a black energy that took root within her. She married an emotionally disconnected man and went on to have three more children, all of whom were given names that began with the same letter, while my dad, whose name wasn't even close to theirs, was an outcast. My father, a brilliant artist, begged to go to art school, but was told he could not, so he enlisted in the Army at a very young age. Later, his parents allowed his youngest brother to enroll in the art school that he so sorely had wanted to attend, a point of contention that I believe sat like lead in my dad. His grandparents, however, adored him and raised him for many years in Florida.

My grandmother would take my siblings on trips to Disney World while I was left home. She would pick my cousins and me up for a shopping trip. After choosing cartloads of new clothes for my cousins, she would tell me that she didn't have any money to buy me anything. However, it was the one day she had picked me up, with my cousins in tow, to take us out for ice cream that hurt me the most. My grandmother ordered an ice cream for everybody but me. When it came to my order, she looked down and told me that I didn't need one and would have to watch as everybody else enjoyed their sweet treat. I tried to hold back my tears. It wasn't that I wanted ice cream so badly; it was that I was confused as to why I was singled out to be punished for no apparent reason. When I went home, I hid in my room and sobbed. My mom finally got me to spill out what was wrong, and the visits to my grandmother were immediately stopped.

My mom was already raw with emotion from the argument and angry at my father, and even more furious with him for calling his mother. She now felt ganged up on.

"What are you doing here?" she asked my grandmother.

"You need help. Mental help."

My mom ran past her mother-in-law to the kitchen and down the basement steps. My grandmother and father followed at a brisk pace. I crept down the stairwell to see my mom hiding behind the dryer and crying. She screamed, "Stop it, just stop it. Leave me alone." But they didn't. They grabbed her, dragging her up the steps, out the back door, and into the car.

My sister grabbed on to me as I sobbed, crying for my mom like any six-year-old would. Although I loved my dad, he was a typical military man who rarely showed emotion. He went to work, came home, sat in front of the television while my mom served him dinner, and then went to bed. My mom, even with her depression and sadness, would read me stories, or at least talk about her childhood or the military travels she had with my dad. I felt as if Alto and Tallie let me down. My dad and grandmother let me down. And now my mom let me down.

As if I hadn't felt like an outcast before, I began first grade with my mom in the psychiatric hospital, her cries etched into my memory forever.

I learned how to read in first grade, a skill that I picked up quickly, and books became my escape from the drama. I closed myself off from everybody at school and from my family—even my father. I look at my first-grade school picture and think what a mess I was with a dress that looked like rags and hair that looked like it hadn't been combed in days. It was a glaring reminder of my absent mom.

During her absence, I felt shut out from the spirit world. Tallie and Alto were there, but I was angry and sad. My sister became my pseudo mom, helping cook dinner for us, and my dad attempted to keep a source of normalcy by going to work, returning home, and waiting for dinner, which had to consist of meat, potatoes, and vegetables, and if bread and dessert was available, all the better.

I wasn't able to visit my mom in the hospital, but my dad would take me to the parking lot, and my mom would wave at me from her fourth-floor window. I politely waved back, as if waving to a long lost relative.

It was several months before we were able to pick up my mom from the psychiatric ward. I sat in the backseat, thinking that for sure she forgot how to love me, and maybe she wouldn't even recognize me. Those months that she was gone, I blamed myself. If I hadn't predicted that death, maybe her mom wouldn't have died. And maybe my mom wouldn't be so sad. And if I wasn't alive, maybe the family would be okay and not so messed up. And maybe it was my entire fault.

My mom climbed into the passenger seat, turned around, and smiled at me. "Hi honey."

I didn't even recognize her. Her personality seemed to change, her energy was different. Although her voice was upbeat, her eyes had lost their sparkle.

I felt utterly and completely alone.

# three

# The Ghost Cottage

As if to try to make up for the last year, my grandmother decided that we should all go on a vacation together and a trip to Ludington, Michigan, which is just a few hours' drive from our home in Detroit, was planned.

My mom, dad, sister, brother, paternal grandmother, and I arrived at the Lake Michigan beach cottage for a week-long getaway. My dad and brother, anxious to put the boat into the water, ran down to take a quick boat ride while the women unpacked the car. Sitting down to catch her breath, my mom glanced at one of the beds and let out a scream.

"I just saw a skull," she gasped.

"What do you mean by that?" my grandmother asked, confused.

"I saw a skeleton head on the bedpost—a skull," my mom repeated, shaking in fright.

My grandmother, ever the cynic, smirked and glanced under the bed. Her large frame sprung to life. "Help me move the bed," she instructed in an urgent tone.

My mom and sister helped push the bed aside to discover an extremely large pool of dried blood. There was no skull found; it was only within my mom's vision.

As quickly as it was pulled away, the bed was pushed back into place and my mom and grandmother were on the phone searching for an alternate vacation spot.

While we waited for the men to return, my sister and I took a walk in the surrounding woods but were stopped just a few feet from the cabin. Hanging from a branch of a large pine tree was a bloodied noose. We ran back to the house as the rest of the party gathered, loaded up the car, and left. From then on, that vacation was referred to as "The Ghost Cottage," and my mom refused to discuss what she saw or how she saw it. The case was closed in her book.

I believe my mom was actually quite gifted, but something in her past had frightened her. Her way of dealing it was to make the subject taboo, effectively shutting down the possibility of helping me with my gift. This gift was part of my fiber—as much as I sometimes begged for it to go away, there was no way to remove it, shut it down, or stop it.

It was the Indian summer after our beach vacation. The house was stifling hot and my dad was at work. We sat on the folding chairs on the small front porch, hoping to catch some breeze. Both my mom and I held a glass of iced water, once in a while taking an ice cube and using it to cool us down.

"Kristy, do you ever see anything good happening?" my mom asked, staring straight forward toward the street.

I thought for a moment. "Just death. I mostly just see death," I responded, holding back tears. I wanted to see happiness. I wanted to see marriages and births, but I mostly just saw death.

"Me too," my mom simply said. She got up and walked back into the house, leaving me to ponder what it all meant.

# four

# My Guardian

My mom received a phone call on a warm August afternoon informing her that her father, my insightful and well-loved grandpa, had been rushed to the hospital. He had been found badly bruised and lying on the floor next to his bed, wallet next to him, but nothing taken. It was uncertain if he'd had a stroke or been beaten up. Being only seven years old, I was quickly shuttled over to our neighbors' home, who we lovingly referred to as Uncle Bill and Aunt Ernie, while the family went to visit the man his friends called "Red." That night, my mom told me that my grandpa kept asking for me. He said he had something very important to tell me. At that time, kids under the age of sixteen weren't allowed in the intensive care unit, and since my grandpa was in awful shape and his face quite bruised and beaten, my mom told me that she didn't think it was a good idea. She added that perhaps my grandfather was delusional because most of what he said didn't make sense; however, she never expanded on that. I begged her to take me to see him, and, more than likely just to get me to stop insisting, she said she would think about it. Unfortunately, there would be no time to think it over as my grandfather passed away, leaving the whole family heartbroken. We did know, however, that his wife and two sons in heaven had to be excited to be reunited with him.

I don't recall seeing him in his casket, but I remember what happened at the cemetery as if it were yesterday.

The gravesite was under a large pine tree next to the cemetery's dirt road. As the mourners said their goodbyes, I could see a shadow of a man who resembled my grandfather standing a couple hundred feet away. He was leaning against the tree and smoking a cigarette, smiling at me. I wiped my tears away and slowly walked over to get a closer look. There was no doubt in my mind that the man standing in the shadows was my grandfather.

Maybe he was alive! Maybe they were wrong and he hadn't died and had just been released from the hospital! It had to be a mistake, right? He was standing right there. I was hugging him and I was wide awake. Maybe they were wrong.

"I'm gone, Kristy," he affirmed, as if sensing my question—aware of my hope, my wish. "But I wanted to talk to you, Kristy. I couldn't leave without talking to you!"

I gulped back tears, knowing that he really was dead, and although I was afraid, I was also excited to be able to see him just as he was when he was alive: solid.

"I know, Kristy. I know about your gift because you and I have a lot in common. I just want to let you know that no matter what..." He stopped, put his cigarette down to his side, and looked me in the eyes. "No matter what, you must not be afraid. You're special, and I will always be there with you to help protect you."

I nodded, unable to speak.

"Take care of your momma," Grandpa added as he began to walk toward his gravesite, only to dissipate into the landscape.

I raced after his spirit, but he had already crossed.

I didn't have the heart to tell my mom that I saw Grandpa; she was too busy with her own grieving. My brother and sister learned to attribute my spirit contact to my "imagination," and I didn't want to be mocked. So, what I did was stuff the message and, instead of being thrilled that someone knew my secret, other than my grandpa who had passed on, I was angry. Why was I left to deal with this curse alone? All I wanted to do was fit into the world and, as if it weren't difficult enough being a kid, I was given *this*.

*This* felt like an ugly birthmark that might be able to be masked with makeup but would still be there no matter what. I went into the closet, literally and figuratively. It was just too much to handle, but it didn't mean that the angels, my guides, loved ones, and random spirits no longer bothered me. They did. But I made a deal that they couldn't call on me unless it was something extremely important; otherwise they would have to wait until I went into the closet.

From the very beginning, I was too sensitive and often called a crybaby. Because I was made fun of so much, I withdrew, attempting to find some solace away from others' emotions. I tried to stay in the shadows as much as I could. I wasn't mentioning the many spirits in the house, and decided that it would be best to go into the closet—literally and figuratively. I would go into the small white-slatted closet in my mom and dad's bedroom and talk to the good spirits. Their bedroom was on the first floor, where there were always good spirits, but the second floor, where my bedroom was, well that was another story. And the basement…the basement was plain evil. I felt the safest place, and where I could peacefully speak with my angels and guides, was the closet.

The tiny, white-slatted closet in my mom and dad's bedroom was stuffed with my mom's clothes (and boy, did she love clothes). The floor was storage for linens, and I fit perfectly on top of them. I'd close the closet door and allow the dead to come and speak to me. It was a bit like a confessional, I suppose. They'd tell me their stories and how they tried to help on this earth, and I'd listen and offer suggestions. They tried to reassure me that I was perfectly sane and had a special purpose, but I felt anything but special. I felt like a freak. Every time I got into that closet, I hoped and prayed that nobody would know what I was actually doing. Nobody ever did. I cried a lot in the closet, but it was a healing cry, because although I'd go in there feeling lonely, I came out feeling supported and loved. I always felt a sense of reassurance as I hid my sobs in my hands, hearing from my guides and angels that one day I would feel accepted and to just be patient.

I was to start third grade just a day after my grandfather's funeral. The teacher, Mr. Brauer, was rumored to be a tyrant. Not only was he a teacher, he was the choir director and organist for the church that was next to the school. I was petrified. My second-grade teacher had been a lovely lady who had seen my sensitive ways and nurtured them with hugs, patience, and love. But Mr. Brauer had a booming voice, swore in German, and had a reputation for pulling ears, smacking with rulers, and generally intimidating his students. I didn't know what to expect, except the rumors that if you did a math problem wrong you would be beaten. If you looked at me the wrong way I would cry, so I was frightened.

My mom didn't have a driver's license, so I would walk to school each day with her, and then back home. The entire walk on that first day of school, I cried. Every step that I took, my fears felt exaggerated.

Prior to Grandpa's death, if my mom wasn't feeling well, and that was often, he would pick me up from school, and I would hop in the front seat. Back then you didn't have to wear seat belts and there weren't rules as to where the kids sat. I felt like a grownup sitting next to him in that big old car.

"What did you learn today, Kristy?" he would ask me each time. My answer was always the same: "Nothing."

"Well, that's a lot of money your parents are spending for you to learn nothing."

I would simply shrug.

The realization that my grandpa wouldn't ever pick me up again began to heighten my anxiety of the first day of school. Maybe I should have talked more to him instead of being snooty. Maybe I should've told him that the kids picked on me or that I was last to be chosen for gym class again because I was so scrawny. Or maybe I should've told him how I worried about my mom and dad. Or that I could see his family on the Other Side around him every time I was with him. It was when I was with him that I felt the closest to God. There were so many regrets.

As we walked up to the side door of the school, the tears became uncontrollable sobs. On the first day of school, the teachers would come and meet their class by the entrance, and I was certainly making a spectacle of myself in front of the entire school and all of the parents, but once the tears started, I couldn't stop them. Through my watery eyes I could see Mr. Brauer walking toward us. All I could do was look down at the ground, and I could see his polished brown leather shoes as they stopped in front of my mom. I prepared myself for the worst. I heard my mom explain that my grandpa had just died and tell him that I was a shy and sensitive child besides. He knelt down to my eye level, took my hand from my mom's, and said, "C'mon Krissy, I'll take good care of you," and walked me into the school, to the classroom and right to my desk. He smiled (he rarely smiled), squeezed my hand in reassurance, and left me to put my supplies away. His gruff and ornery reputation was quickly replaced with the loving teddy bear that was his true nature. He continued to call me Krissy throughout the years and he helped give me a voice, a singing voice. He would often give me solos and he encouraged me to sign up for the talent shows. When there were auditions for the Broadway show *Annie*, he was the first one to tell me that I needed to take a chance and try out. And I did. This shy little girl stood in front of the Big Apple judges and danced and sang. And didn't make it. But the point was that this was the beginning of discovering who I was, and another escape for me that was much more acceptable than talking to imaginary friends.

# five

## Kept Promises

A few months after Grandpa's passing, an incident validated his promise of protecting me and helped to change the course of my life.

I was forced to tag along with my mom and dad to a local mall in Southfield, Michigan. Both of my parents loved to shop, something I've always detested, so when my mom wanted to go into a local clothing store, they allowed me to sit on a bench in front of the fountain with my constant companion, a book. A few minutes after they left, a man came up to me. He was quite tall and had a camera dangling around his neck.

"You're such a beautiful little girl," he said with an English accent. "Mind if I take your picture? I only have a few pictures left, and I really want to get this film developed."

I nodded my head in agreement.

"Just stand right there," he instructed, and I simply stood up in front of where I had been sitting. He put the camera up to his eye and I heard a click.

"Oh, look at how pretty your long blonde hair is," he said, reaching out to touch it. "Let's go outside and get some better photos; that way the sun can shine through your hair."

Sensing my anxiety, he gently took hold of my elbow. "It will only take a moment," he said reassuringly, with a hard smile on his face.

I was a polite little girl, and, although I sensed something was awry, the moments happened too quickly for a reaction. We walked a few steps toward the door when I smelled my grandpa—that heavy cigarette smell that permeated his skin. I heard grandpa yell "Run!" in my ear, and without hesitation I turned and bolted before the man could get a better grip on me. I ran as hard as I could, not looking back even once. I sensed the large hands of my grandfather pushing me gently away from the kidnapper. Out of breath, crying, and frightened, I found my parents at the checkout line. I tried to explain what happened, but by the time my dad returned to the mall area, the man with the camera was gone.

Weeks after the attempted kidnapping, I begged my parents to allow me to get my hair cut. I made the excuse that I was tired of the long tangled locks, but subconsciously I saw my long hair as a threat to my life. After all, it was the hair that the man said he was drawn to. My hair was chopped off in a short bob that I detested, but I smiled through my tears and got my ears pierced so that I wouldn't be mistaken for a boy.

Years later I realized what had almost happened to me and recognized that my grandfather possibly saved my life. It was during that exact same year that a string of child killings gripped the community. Being so young, I was oblivious to the news story, but my neighborhood was on high alert to a serial killer. Was it the Oakland County Killer, a person who the new stations referred to as "The Babysitter" because each of his victims were fed and washed thoroughly before being dumped? Had it been him that attempted to lure me just as he did all four found victims? Or was my would-be abductor just another sick individual? I may never know, but what I do know is that my grandfather, in spirit, saved my life. Our loved ones stay with us, by our sides, when we call upon them or when we most need them. They are never far.

Although I didn't know the gravity of what could've happened, I was well aware that Grandpa was around me when I needed him most. That experience helped me become an advocate for missing and murdered children cases, using my gift to help in any way possible. And although Alto and Tallie were still around, it was as if they knew I needed the comfort of my grandpa.

After the near miss, I moved on from Nancy Drew mysteries and became obsessed with true crime books, serial killers, and the psychological profile that made up these individuals. I would consider the crime and, by using the visions and images my guides gave me, attempt to figure out the whodunit as I read the books. With my diary, a pen, and the book, I spent hours writing down the symbols and clues that made up the visions that would be shown in my head. What was the weapon? If a gun, I would feel the gunshot; if a knife, the slash to my skin. Was the perpetrator male or female? With a male, I would feel a heavier feeling than the softer feel of a female. It became almost a game of charades that helped decipher the messages. What month did it happen? Was it cold or hot? Did I see an Easter lily or a Christmas tree? I realized I could hear, feel, smell, and see, and not just see in my mind's eye—I could actually see the spirits just as if they were still flesh and blood. It became a bit of a game in order to decipher the clues, but it was something much more serious than a game. It was real. It would become my life. It is my life.

# six

# The Haunting

The house I grew up in was a small Victorian in Detroit, Michigan, with two bedrooms upstairs and an added bedroom on the first floor. I shared an upstairs bedroom with my older sister, and my brother had the room next to ours.

Because my siblings were so much older than me, I grew up as if I were an only child and was very spoiled, not only because my parents were financially stable, but because after raising two kids, they were confident enough to have a laidback parenting style.

I didn't really have a bedtime and would much rather fall asleep with all of the lights on—I was even comforted when it was still light outside. This was because nighttime was when spirits were free to roam, at least in that home, and because they knew I could see them, it was also a freefor-all for them to tease and abuse me at will. Different from those that consoled me in the closet, these spirits were dark, evil even. Every night I raced as fast as I could to get into bed, sure that something was going to reach out and grab me. All the closets had to stay open, every light had to be on, and I still shook with fear. I didn't have to explain what to do because in my family's eyes none of it was real and I was just looking for attention. I'd stay awake as long as I could, sometimes until morning. This went on until I moved out of the house when I was nineteen.

The worst part of the house was the basement. It was dimly lit, and although spotlessly clean, I just knew that something bad had happened underneath the stairway in a previous time. I'd be near tears if I had to go down to get the laundry. Once again, my family thought I was over-dramatizing, but as soon as I reached the third stair down, I could feel the watchful eyes of an entity that lived off of my fear and the negative energy that stood stagnate from past transgressions. It was a large, looming dark shadow that could teleport in an instant. The anticipation of what it could do, or what it was, frightened me. But it was the year that my dad began bringing home books on Aleister Crowley and demons that I stopped sleeping upstairs for good and slept on the living room couch.

My dad wasn't worshiping Satan, but was teaching courses on the occult at our local church. Unfortunately, the portals already existing in the home, combined with the beacon of light that shone from me as if saying hey, this girl can see, hear, and feel you, amplified the activity. My brother would feel strangled by invisible hands after settling into bed. Objects would disappear, only to reappear in odd locations. The overall feeling of the house felt dark and dreary. One of the things that frightened my mom to death was birds. It didn't matter what kind or how big or small they were, she didn't like the sound of wings flapping. As my mom's sight worsened, the issue with the birds did, too. It was always a crow or a raven, and we could never figure out how they got into the home, but we knew that they came from the basement. Always. And since that was her sign for death, as she had explained to me when my grandma passed away, it fueled her anxiety, and she silently wondered who else was going to be taken from her. The birds always found their way up from the basement and flapped around the house while my mom cowered, arms over her head, screaming for me to get help.

Help came in the form of our elderly and very grumpy next-door neighbor, a lady we called Aunt Ernie. She'd grab her broom and sweep the birds out, yelling, "Sally, it's just a bird!" Regardless, the birds stirred up the nightmares in Mom's mind and, without being able to actually see the birds' flight patterns, it was like living in a horror house for her. For me too, but I could also *see*. It wasn't just birds; it was also infestations of bugs, ants, flying ants, and beetle-like insects that we would find in all parts of the house—even when it was cold and nothing should've been surviving. My parents would call critter-control companies, but they could never figure out where the birds or the bugs were coming from. It was a mystery to the experts, and I didn't know that we were seeking the wrong experts. We needed a minister, a priest, a medium, or all of the above. Not only were the birds wandering in mysteriously to frighten us, but the bugs would find their way into the home, and there were the ghosts that stood there, staring at us as we tried to sleep. Nobody else could see them, but I could see them, but I couldn't do anything about it.

It wasn't until I began embracing my psychic gift and researching both the light and the darkness of the unknown, along with networking with those who embraced the different worlds, that it dawned on me that my mom's depression and her many undiagnosed ailments weren't merely manifestations of genetics, but that the monsters that lived within that childhood home had sought either her, me, or both of us to take advantage of our empathic gifts. She didn't know how to block it, as she was either frightened or completely unaware of what was going on. The energies I hated so much fed off of my mom, leaving us with only pieces of what had been a beautiful soul.

Every once in a while I tried sharing messages with Mom, hoping her response would be different. I hoped that messages from her family members in spirit would offer her some happiness. But instead of it making her feel surrounded by their love, she felt sad and lonesome, so I stopped sharing. It was easier to withdraw into the spook closet than to face the looks that I received.

The energies in the home only got worse after my dad took me to a local church to listen to a Presbyterian minister who did missionary work in Third World countries. His specialty was exorcism.

My dad was intensely studying the Bible at that time, and he was curious about the darker realm. With tape recorder in tow, we sat down in the pew to listen and watch video of a documentary.

I can't remember the lecturer's name, but even though I was only in the fourth grade, I found the man charismatic and not at all what I thought a demon hunter would be like. He began his lecture and then stopped after about ten minutes in.

"I forgot to pray," he gasped. "We must pray in order to protect ourselves and to ask God to allow the recordings to work."

The man said a quick prayer and then began again. The lecture, probably no more than an hour long, was absolutely fascinating for even a nine-year-old. When we got home, my dad rewound the cassette tape and hit play. We heard moans of unknown origin; to this day, thinking back to those sounds makes me cringe and feel ill. After about ten minutes of howls, cries, and moans, we heard the minister loudly say "amen," and then the tape played perfectly.

Just a few nights after that lecture, I awoke to a man's voice distinctly coming through the radio. He called my name and laughed at my fright. I recited the Lord's Prayer, asking him to go away, but it continued over and over. I was afraid to get out of my bed, so I sat there, wide-eyed and crying. He finally stopped and I raced down the steps into my parents' bedroom. By this time, they were aggravated with my bogey-men stories and just pointed to the couch.

My brother came home late from his job and went to sleep in his bedroom. It wasn't long after calling it a night that he too, at twenty-one years of age, raced down the steps yelling that something was walking on his bed and it felt as if something was strangling and choking him. Chaos unfolded after that. Knives began disappearing from the utensil drawer, only to be found buried, point up, in our backyard. Rocks would be thrown at our home from the alley in back, and yet nobody was there. The final episode came when our furnace stopped working and my dad went downstairs to look at it. He yelled up that the pilot light had blown out. Although I was ill that day and lay on the couch, weakened by the virus, I had an awful feeling and yelled out for him not to do anything, but it was too late—the explosion gave my dad severe burns on his arm and face, and he was rushed to the hospital. The repairman said that the dial on the furnace was turned all the way up, but my dad denied touching anything, and nobody else had been down there. There wasn't any other explana-tion, and without a word, the books on anything occult were taken out back and burned. After injuring my dad, the evil hibernated. The basement still felt creepy, but I didn't sense anybody down there anymore. The infesta-tion of birds and bugs stopped, and the shadows that I continually saw slithering up and down the stairwell were few and far between. And so the feeling of evil seemed to hibernate, but I still hated that house. I felt as if something would happen again, but I didn't know what, when, or how. To stay away from the house, I signed up for every type of after-school activity that I could so I wouldn't get home until it was time to lay my head on the pillow on the couch. My clothes were still in my bedroom closet and I would grab my outfit and change in the bathroom, but always still feeling watched.

I realized early on that it was easier to keep my spirit friends hidden from the family, but while doing that I concealed my true self. I stayed in the spook closet, physically and emotionally. At least I tried to. It seemed that I was what I now refer to as a ghost magnet. I put my attention on hating the home we lived in, thinking it to be spooky with hidden secrets. In retrospect it wasn't the house, but the energy that ran amok there. It's the same energy that I blame for stealing my mom's hope, her health, and ultimately, her eyesight.

One of the signs and symptoms of having a negative or demonic energy in the home is depression and oppression. Many attribute it to full-blown possession by the demonic energy, and, although that can occur, it is rare. It's much easier for the energy to just cause chaos around those in the home instead of exerting the energy to possess the inhabitants. After the lecture, this situation got worse.

The negative presence in the house had already driven me to sleep on the itchy brown plaid couch in the living room, just feet away from my mom and dad's bedroom. The taunting, nightmares, and scary feelings were just about driving me mad and all I wanted was to have the sanctuary of my own bedroom, but there was no haven in my home. When I wasn't busy with after-school activities or dance classes, my only escape was when my nose was in a book. Only then could I ignore the stress of my mom's illnesses, the stress of my sister's drama, and the stress of my dad trying to hide from the stress. All of the emotions were a beacon to the negative energy that wanted to feed, and I was the target, or so my ego felt that way. In essence, the whole family was. I prayed every night that a miracle would occur, and we would move. To me, moving away from the negative was my hope that my mom would get better and that my sister would find her way home. It wasn't until later, after working similar paranormal cases, that I realized that the negative would've followed, but to my nine-year-old brain and happily-ever-after heart and soul I saw it as an answer. The answer.

I made my bed on the couch, as I had for several years, even though I had a large room on the second floor colored in purple paint with a canopy bed. I instead opted for the uncomfortable wool couch and knowing that my parents were just a yell away.

I had just fallen asleep when I awoke to find myself drifting. I could touch the ceiling. I looked down to see my physical body on the couch, sleeping peacefully, and felt at that moment that if I didn't pull myself back to my body that I would die and drift away—far away. I could see in the distance, something farther than the ceiling itself, a white energy, and knew that the energy was going "home" and I felt sad and lonely. I panicked and pulled myself down on to my physical body, took a deep breath, and jerked myself awake. My heart beat fast and I felt as if I had just died and come back to life. I felt someone watching me over my shoulder and swung around to see a young girl. She had long curly blonde hair and wore all white. It was a white that I had never seen before. It didn't just sparkle—it emitted a sense of pureness and love. Her face was round, her cheeks rosy, and she spoke to me telepathically. "You are loved, Kristy. You are safe, Kristy." Instead of asking questions or starting any sort of communication (something I regret to this day), I leaped off the couch and ran right through her and into my mom and dad's room, where they simply allowed me to snuggle with them until I fell back asleep.

I had stopped talking to anybody about my strange happenings long ago, but I was shaken and so I confided to my mom. She turned ashen, and before I fully described to her what the little girl looked like, my mom described her to me—right down to the lace on her sleeves. She said she had a dream about her that night where the girl told her she would lose a child, and she began to tear up thinking perhaps it was a premonition of my own death, but I shared the message with her: "You are loved, Kristy. You are safe, Kristy." That afternoon, my mom miscarried a baby that she wasn't even aware she was carrying. She called me into the bathroom to help her call the doctor, and we both cried with sadness at the loss, yet also relief that it wasn't my death that I witnessed, but my sister's death. No, I don't know for sure that the baby was a girl, but both my mom and I had a *knowing* that it was.

# seven

# Shadows of Darkness

My family, as dysfunctional as most, was never the Sunday-night-dinner type when I was young and never became that as we grew, but we always got together for the holidays and we "kids" all had a close relationship with our mom and dad.

Mom was not a hypochondriac, but, for as long as I could remember, she suffered from various physical ailments and they only multiplied after she lost her father. My mom's depression, the result of losing her entire family in a span of several years, began to take a toll on her physically and her eyesight began to deteriorate.

It was Christmas when we first noticed. Mom was always particular about clothes, and when I saw that the clothes she bought as gifts and what she had paired them with didn't match, I thought perhaps she was just branching out. When I thanked her for the blue shirt and orange socks, she looked appalled. "Orange? Aren't those socks blue?" Even after subsequent years of doctor appointments, nobody could properly diagnose her illness or offer hope. She never adjusted to the blindness and fought hard when various services tried to help her adapt. Instead, she slipped into a heavy depression, which affected us all. Her blindness prevented her from doing a variety of things, and her self-pity made me cry and turn it into my own self-pity. I wanted her to one day read a book I'd authored. I wanted her to help me choose a wedding dress and see me walk down the aisle. I wanted her to see what her grandchildren would look like and show off their pictures. I wanted her to show me how to apply makeup. I wanted her to cook me my favorite dish from her kitchen: chicken noodle soup. I wanted my mom—my whole mom and not just the shell of her.

My mom fell into a deep depression when her mom passed, and when her best friend and father passed away when I was eight years old, her depression lent itself to a mountain of health issues, including color blindness. When I was twelve years old, she lost her sight completely.

She hopped from doctor to specialist, to psychiatrist and doctor again, to finally be diagnosed with lupus and put on heavy medication, which accentuated her already deep depression. We were grateful for an answer, but a year later, the physicians said that she was misdiagnosed, yet didn't have any answers again. We had hoped that it was just macular degeneration, but that too was ruled out. The doctors were stumped. They explained that it was as if her retinas were completely eaten away, and that the disease she had was rare, only a few thousand cases in the world, and it was genetic and there was no cure. They called it retinitis pigmentosa; they weren't completely certain that was the proper diagnosis, but they needed to call it something. The name of the blindness didn't matter to any of us—we just knew that in the end, my mom would never ever see again.

# eight

## *Watchtower*

A field that sat far back from my school was used for the outdoor gym class. It was nicknamed "the cornfield" as it had once been farmland. The cornfield overlooked a major street in Detroit called Grand River. With only a chain-link fence separating us from the outside world, I often sat outside the fence and lost myself in daydreams.

The soccer game was in full swing, and my teacher called me to join the team. Reluctantly, I ran in. I wasn't an athletic child, but instead was what could be referred to as a delicate runt, so it wasn't odd for my classmates to run around me instead of play with me. Yes, I was the one who was always chosen last in gym and who cowered in the corner during dodgeball, begging to be mercifully hit so I could sit out the rest of the game, but this day was most unusual. As I pretended to play, I immediately felt as if I were taken outside my body and put into another time.

*I knew that my name was Debby and I was a runaway teenager. I sat on the torn-up vinyl seat of a dirty blue Buick. The thirty-something Caucasian man sitting beside me was scrubby looking and smelled awful. He had promised he would protect me. I didn't want to be with my mom and dad, and even though I was hungry and sad, it had to be better than home. My parents were constantly fighting and didn't care anyway. They probably didn't even know that I was missing. The man told me that he had to stop for a second and parked his car near a field. He got out of the car. I watched him take a deep breath, put his hands on his head, and then come over to my side of the car. Before I could react, he grabbed me and pulled me down beside the car. He roughly pulled down my pants. I screamed. He smacked me hard against the side of the mouth, and I could feel blood rolling down my cheek, toward my right ear. I whimpered as he continued to hold me down and rape me. I closed my eyes and prayed, "God, I'm so sorry. Please, Mommy and Daddy, please, I'm so sorry. Please let someone find me. Please help me."*

"Kristy!" Someone was screaming my name.

I had fallen to the ground, sobbing.

"Kristy, what's wrong?" my sixth-grade teacher asked me.

I shook my head and looked around. I was back in the cornfield with my classmates and everyone was looking at me as if I were crazy.

"I think a bee stung me on my leg," I quickly answered. I knew I shouldn't lie, but I didn't know how to explain what I had just experienced and not be checked into the funny farm.

"Okay, run to the bathroom and let me know if we should call your parents."

My mom and I always had a pretty good relationship, at least before I reached my teenage years. I could tell her just about anything and she didn't judge, but I was always afraid of discussing the visions I saw, the feelings that I had, and the things that I just knew. I had tried early on, and I could tell that she was uncomfortable. From an early age, I loved reading horoscopes, but if I read hers aloud, she'd tell me to put it away—and that I shouldn't read stuff like that. I never questioned why she felt the way she did; I felt it was easier to ignore. But that day had me shaken up, and, of course, there was a note that went home that told of the incident and a possible bee sting, so I had to tell her. I felt the truth was the best way anyhow.

Mom didn't judge me that day and instead reacted with concern. I'm sure she was taken aback that an eleven-year-old experienced a rape, and yet she was confused as to how to deal with it since the rape victim wasn't really me. She asked if I thought the girl had been murdered. It was a question that still bothers me. I didn't know. I didn't think so, but I didn't know for sure.

The visions I received were unpredictable, but constant. I could be walking through a grocery store, pick up a jar of peanut butter, and see the image of a grandmother dying from cancer, her family standing all around her and praying for her soul's safe journey. Or I might talk to a teacher about an assignment, only to be shown an image of her cheating on her spouse. It became a constant chatter in my head that didn't stop, and it was all bad. I wasn't seeing babies being born, job promotions, or happy news. I saw only death and darkness. I couldn't prevent it. I was no superhero who could change bad things to good, so why was I seeing all this? Was I being punished by witnessing such awful things? It wasn't until later when I explored that same question that I realized it was because I was allowing the dark to envelop me. I concentrated on the dark, and the more I was angry about it, the more darkness shrouded the light.

It became apparent then that it wasn't just the house—it was much deeper and darker than that. It was also *me.*

I loved people, and still do, but I just couldn't seem to have a close friend in school. I'd ask classmates to come over and spend the night, but they'd rarely agree. I was asked several times to sleep over at their homes, but I wanted to also have them at my house. Even though I hated my house, I wanted a sense of normalcy. I'd sit at my desk and look out the windows that faced the street and cry out for a true friend.

For my tenth birthday, my mom agreed to let me have a sleepover.

"But you have to sleep in your room, Kristy," she warned.

Of course! There was no way I was going to let on that I was ten years old and sleeping on my living room couch! Yes, my room scared me, but I rationalized that it was because the entity liked to terrorize me. And for sure there had to be safety in numbers—even when it came to the paranormal.

I invited four girls and they all agreed to come. I was thrilled. I cleaned my room, was all dressed up, and was ready for the party. It was within hours of the girls' arrival that one by one each of them became ill and had to go home. I called them later that night to see how they were, and they all sounded fine and said they felt better. I felt so completely depressed. My mom held me as I cried, wondering why nobody liked me. My mom cried too, feeling my pain, wishing she could remove it.

What I didn't know, and wouldn't until years later when reuniting with my classmates, was that it wasn't me they didn't want to be with, it was that my house made them sick. They too saw the shadows, heard the footsteps, and felt the swirling, unstable energy within the house. I wish they would've let me in on it then and wonder if feeling validated would have changed anything for me.

Visions, nightmares, sickness, demons, ghosts: it wasn't a dreamy childhood, but later on it would help me help others enduring the same or similar torments.

# nine

## *Sensitive*

I was excited to go to high school and even more excited that my so-called curse was at a gentle hum instead of the roar. It could've been that I was so busy with activities and was so rarely home that I just couldn't be affected by it, or it was simply hormones. Any which way, life was starting to be as normal as I could wish for. Even though I was once again enrolled in a Lutheran facility, there was a sense of independence. After being stuck for nine years at the grade school (kindergarten through eighth grade), the change was very much needed. We were given the choice of going to two high schools, Lutheran West or Lutheran Northwest. West was more sports oriented and Northwest more artistic. I chose Northwest. A new start, a new beginning.

It was the middle of my sophomore year when we received word that Lutheran West would be closing, Lutheran

Northwest would be relocating its campuses, and a new building would open in Westland, which was nearer to me than either school. It was hard to say goodbye to the classmates I thought I would be graduating with and even harder to say goodbye to my best friend who decided to go to public school. So, junior year was another chance for new beginnings and I set out to make it the best ever. I decided that even though I felt that I was uncoordinated, I was going to try out for everything from cheerleading to basketball to drama, and seemed to be hitting the jackpot as I became captain of both cheerleading and basketball teams and received roles in the drama productions. The school was small, though, and it was determined that the junior class (my class) would be top dogs for two years straight as they didn't want to transfer a senior class. This provided lots of opportunities to build close relationships. Just a week into the first semester, a boy kept trying to catch my eye. He was outgoing, flirtatious, and gave no apologies for his aggressiveness. He was also a star football player and all-state wrestler, and I wasn't at all interested, and yet I was drawn to him for some reason. One of my teachers who had come over from my previous school pulled me aside after school and asked me if I had known that boy beforehand. I shook my head no. He gave me a puzzled look and said that the moment he met me he felt that he had known me all his life, maybe even lifetimes before, and he had the same feeling with my suitor. I laughed at him. Past lifetimes? What was a Lutheran teacher talking about past lifetimes for? Nonsense! He gave me a sideways look as if trying to see into the past and perhaps even the future, and warned me to be careful. He shook his head as if trying to remove the memory and went on his way. Just a few weeks after, that boy and I were inseparable, with only one problem—my boyfriend's mother didn't much like me. She pretended she did, but her smiles seemed forced, her smirks not as hidden as she thought. I came from the wrong side of the tracks, so to speak. My dad worked for Ford Motor Company (in the factory) and we lived in Detroit. Although I was motivated to become something, I knew I wasn't what she thought her boy should have. I should've taken her disapproval as a sign.

Along with having a boyfriend and my constant after-school activities, I also started working at Kmart. It wasn't too far from home, they paid well, and they were flexible with my school schedule, but the problem was that every time I had an exchange with a customer, I would get the feelings or images in my head and I wasn't sure how to handle it.

One of my most powerful experiences came when a family, two children and their parents, went through my line. They had somber looks on their faces and, as I rang up their items, I kept smelling smoke. The mom handed me her credit card and I got an image of an older lady choking, smoke swirling all around her, and then death. I tried to suppress it, but began to cough uncontrollably. I grabbed my water to try to take a sip, but that only made it worse. My manager came over, told me to go back to the break room, and completed the transaction. When I returned to my register, I noticed that the family had left, but the mom was waiting for me.

She pulled me aside and asked if I was okay. I just nodded, tears in my eyes, but playing it off as if it was just my choking. She asked me if I saw things, and, again, I just nodded. I was only sixteen years old and still confused about this so-called gift. The lady informed me that they were on their way to her mother's funeral. Two days previous, her mom had fallen asleep with a cigarette and died in the fire. I had relived her mother's passing. We exchanged hugs and she left. The manager looked at me as if I had grown an extra ear, and I figured that it wasn't much use to attempt to explain. After all, I wasn't quite certain how to explain it anyhow.

My mom was sensitive in emotion also and she could feel my emotion without me vocalizing it, or even being in the same room. Instead of comforting me, she'd get wrapped up in the depression of a passed-on family member, or in mysterious health issues that would pop up. Her health issues ranged from aching everywhere to stomach issues and finally to complete blindness. It wasn't until much later that I understood that the sensitivity had a name. Mom was an empath. I was an *empath*.

Being an empath has to be one of the most misunderstood and underacknowledged gifts under the psychic ability umbrellas. It's feeling others' pain and not quite knowing how to assist. Have you ever walked into a room and just felt this overpowering anger, or sadness, or even happiness and didn't have a clue why your mood changed so quickly? We could call it Psychic Bipolarism.

Empaths weren't mainstreamed until the science fiction TV series *Star Trek: The Next Generation* introduced the character Deanna Troi, who had the ability to sense emotion. Although a fictional program, it helped those experiencing similar abilities to feel a sense of acceptance.

Empaths are also called Sensitive, as those with this ability are more sensitive in all aspects—emotional and physical, conscious and subconscious—and can pick up on everything around them, everything from disapproval to sadness to happiness.

I continued to work retail, but would often go home in tears. My boyfriend, who didn't know how to handle my sadness, stood by my side, and I was thrilled when, at nineteen years old, he got on bended knee and asked me to marry him.

# ten

## Illusions

It was just a few weeks after my twenty-first birthday when we said our vows in a beautiful church wedding on December 7. (Yes, we married on Pearl Harbor Day—a prediction for what our marriage would turn out to be.) It was a very happy day and we danced the night away, glowing in the romance of it all.

My husband didn't understand what I was, and as time continued his tolerance of my sensitivity made him angrier and angrier. If he looked at me the wrong way, I'd sob. Instead of reassuring me, he'd let his anger boil and I'd sulk in the fairy tale that I so badly wanted and had possibly written in my head. High school sweethearts. Captain of the football team with the captain of the cheerleading squad. Sickening sweet, but with a hidden, darker side.

I lay in a bed in the emergency room when a pastor, doctor, and social worker came in. I was having horrible abdominal pain and had just been put through the wringer of numerous medical tests.

"Is your husband beating you, Kristy?" the minister asked.

"What? No!"

"Explain the three fractured ribs then," the doctor said, holding up the X-ray.

I burst into laughter. I had completely forgotten about that morning at Aikido class when my husband playfully football-tackled me. They didn't believe me, but they released me to him anyhow. A few days later I became violently ill, only to receive a call from the hospital that I was pregnant. The morning sickness became all-day sickness and incapacitated me most of my pregnancy. My husband wasn't thrilled with the pregnancy coming so soon after our marriage, but there was no way that I was going to get rid of the baby. The constant illness didn't help our relationship. I developed preeclampsia in the second trimester of my pregnancy, which resulted in either making the trip down to the hospital in Detroit to be monitored or bed rest at home—all while trying to stay employed.

I was five months pregnant with my firstborn when my grandmother, who was hospitalized and dying, called and left me a voice mail. She was sobbing and asking for my forgiveness. She asked that I call her so we could reconcile. I felt perhaps it was her way of looking for the golden ticket to the Other Side, so I decided to hold off on a reply. She passed away that same night. She was buried with many secrets—except for one. On her deathbed, she informed my dad that she had not been raped at all, and offered my dad his father's name.

There are many days that I regret not getting back to her, giving her one last chance to explain herself, to explain why she treated me with such discord, but too much hurt had built up. I believe I grew resentful and bitter for not having a typical warm and loving grandmother. At the wedding to my children's father, she bad-mouthed me to my boss and anybody else who would listen, claiming that I was the most spoiled person she had ever met. Maybe I was, but I just wanted to be loved, and maybe she did, too.

It was August 10 and I was eight months pregnant when I developed a terrible headache—every time my head pounded I saw different colored lights, as if angels of all different colors were singing a message to me. I called the doctor's office and left a message with the answering service. After an hour and no return call, I decided to take a shower and sleep it off. The next morning was my check-up and since I was still feeling lousy, my husband came along. My blood pressure was slightly elevated, but that wasn't unusual—I had gained almost one hundred pounds during the pregnancy, and it was an excruciatingly hot and humid summer. Although Micaela wasn't due until the second week of September, the obstetrician said that if she didn't come before August 23, he would induce on that date. The problem was she was breach and facing backward. I'd had enough of being pregnant and was near tears as I climbed down from the table. "Oh, by the way, why did you call yesterday?" the doctor inquired. He said he tried calling back, but nobody answered. When I told him about the headache, the blood in his face drained and he asked me to take another urine test. In the thirty minutes since I'd come into the office, my protein had doubled. He immediately sent us to the hospital, where I was given a drug that made me feel like water from hell was boiling inside of me and then had an emergency C-section.

On August 11, 1994, we welcomed a baby girl named Micaela. The pregnancy had been awful, as was the delivery. I can now joke that she was truly trying to kill me.

I didn't get the normal bonding time with my baby girl, as I was taken from recovery into the intensive care unit and heavily medicated with what the nurses referred to as hell water, an anticonvulsant medication, magnesium sulfate. I awoke the next day to my husband bringing friends in and making fun of me for talking nonsense, only to fall asleep and wake an hour later to immediately rejoin the conversation as if nothing had happened. My husband thought it was hysterical and kept inviting his friends to the hospital. I became a sideshow as I fell in and out of a medical-induced stupor. I didn't think it was funny and instead it made me sad and hurt.

The second night in intensive care, the heart monitors started to go off. Doctors rushed in to give me an EKG and I passed out. I heard a priest praying over me when I woke up. I surprised him when I asked who he was and informed him that I was Lutheran. When my doctor came to check on me, I asked him what had happened. He told me I didn't need to know, and that I should just rest. I joked that I was probably receiving my last rites. My doctor didn't laugh.

Recovery was slow, but coming home with that baby girl in my arms made everything worth it.

Nine months later I was pregnant again and I had a sinking feeling as I told my husband, who was still adjusting to having Micaela. Intuitively, I was right on the mark. Instead of being excited and passing out cigars, he told me to get rid of the baby or else he was leaving. Now, the signs were right there, but in my head he was still my high school sweetheart, and I wanted the happy family with the two-point-five kids and the picket fence. The problem was that we were young and I was smothering him. Each time I had a feeling he was thinking of straying, I'd panic, which just pushed him away even more. A few days after sharing the news with him (but not the rest of the family), I was at work when I developed awful cramps. I called my doctor's office and was told to get to the hospital quickly because they feared it was an ectopic pregnancy—a case where the embryo develops outside of the uterine cavity. The doctor's staff also told me to call our parents, who only scolded me for not telling them. It wouldn't have made any difference. I lost the babies—twins. I woke up from the anesthesia to see my husband flirting with the recovery room nurse and laughing at me. I was torn up inside, emotionally and physically.

And once again, that should have been a strong sign to leave, but instead I wanted to add to the family with hopes that if our family was complete, we could move on with our lives and rediscover the love. Naïve or a hopeless romantic? Probably more naïvety. I did indeed get pregnant, but just a few weeks after the positive pregnancy test I again developed cramps. This time my doctor sent me for an ultrasound. The look on the technician's face spoke volumes as she excused herself to get a doctor. The doctor patted my hand and told me that I was losing the baby, and I would probably have the miscarriage that night. I did. I shed gallons of tears of frustration because something that was supposed to be natural was so difficult for my body. But for the following three weeks, I continued to have morning sickness and nausea and then had a visit from my grandfather.

We stood in an all-white room. In his arms was a baby wrapped in a blue blanket, and he stretched his arms out for me to take him. I looked into my grandfather's eyes and he telepathically reassured me that everything would unfold the way it was supposed to and that the baby was a gift from him. The next morning I called the doctor.

"I really think I'm still pregnant," I blurted out as soon he came on the phone, without mentioning the visit from my grandpa.

"Kristy, we drew your blood and the levels went down, indicating the loss." His compassion came through in his voice. He had been my OB/GYN since before Micaela and had witnessed the miscarriages, seen the marital issues, and knew that I had a lot of stress in my life.

"Did it go to zero, though?" I inquired. His silence was telling. "Well, did it?"

"No," he sighed. "Tell you what. You get another ultrasound, and if you aren't pregnant, you'll make a deal with me to get some therapy."

"Deal," I said, smiling, certain that I wouldn't have to be sitting on a therapist's couch—at least not for that.

The next day I was back in the same examining room, with the same doctor and technician who had told me I was going to lose the baby. I held my breath and asked my guides, grandparents, and angels to help with the miracle.

"This can't be," the doctor exclaimed. "There's a baby. Not only that, the baby is the same gestational age as the one you lost."

"A twin?" the technician asked.

"We may never know, but there is for sure what looks like a healthy developing baby."

The pregnancy, although it started out rocky, was pretty much normal. The news that it was a boy was also exciting, and I thought perhaps I could win over my husband by giving him a son. It wasn't until I was being wheeled into the operating room for a C-section that we decided on his name: Connor Drake.

I had a premonition awaiting the prep for the C-section and was told by my guides to ask for another. They didn't expand, and I hadn't a clue what "another" was. It wasn't until I was already in the surgery room that I knew exactly what they meant. I was having contractions and was bent over the table as the anesthetist began to insert the needle above my spinal cord, but he missed and tried again, only to miss the second time. The operating room erupted in angry confrontations as I tried to stay still while having contractions and feeling only partially numb. My mind wandered to the fear of feeling the surgery. Finally, the third attempt was a charm.

As I lay in the recovery room, my husband and nurse came to give me the news. Connor was healthy, but he had a cleft palate in the soft palate and was born without a uvula. The hospital wasn't sure what to do with him, and I hadn't a clue what a cleft palate or a uvula even was. Holding my baby boy, he looked as perfect as could be, but once I started to feed him, I realized that he wasn't getting any milk out of the bottle and his frustration was making me teary, which was only compounded by a resident who came in with my chart a couple hours after giving birth.

"Kristy? Can you tell me what you did to make your son this way?"

"Excuse me?"

"Drugs, alcohol...you caused this cleft," the doctor stated with a smirk on his face.

I caused the cleft? Thinking that I did anything that would've hurt my baby made me want to vomit. Had I really caused the cleft? Immediately I fell into a depression, contemplating each and every thing I had put into my system. Was it the ibuprofen after I miscarried? Or the cough medicine I was told would be safe when I had a cold? I've never smoked a cigarette in my life. I never did any drugs and I hated alcohol. I had even quit all caffeine during the pregnancy, but somehow *I* caused the cleft?

After being stunned at the accusation, appalled, I ordered the doctor out of the room. The next doctor who came in informed me that Connor would have to be transferred to a children's hospital. My response was "over my dead body," so they brought the team from the children's hospital to us.

Because of the botched spinal anesthesia, the following morning when I got up to take a shower, I noticed that I couldn't feel my right leg and mentioned it to my nurse and the doctor who came to check up on me, but everybody was so concerned with Connor, and rightfully so, that my concerns went unnoticed. So, I did exactly what I needed to do—I put all of my attention on Connor.

I was now twenty-five years old with two kids under the age of two, and living with a husband who resented me, not only because we now had two children, but because I had also put on a lot of weight. He had threatened previously that if I gained weight, he would divorce me. It was said in fun, but there was an undertone of seriousness. At that point, even though I wasn't happy within myself, I didn't care. All I cared about were the words of that resident, which reverberated through every step of my morning, afternoon, and night: "You caused the cleft." It didn't help when my husband repeatedly told me that the baby must've gotten the problems from my side of the family because, after all, his was perfect.

There was no compassion, only criticism. I became so depressed that I lost my dreams in both daytime and night, unless they had something to do with the kids. I was angry with the world for giving me such a rotten life. Why me? It was a constant question I asked because it was a constant statement I heard growing up with my family. If it wasn't "Why me?" it was "What's next?" I anticipated something bad was about to happen because that was all I was taught to expect.

The next year flew by, filled with surgeries for Connor to repair not only the cleft but also hearing loss that resulted from it. Then there were doctor appointments and physical therapy for my back and leg, as it turned out that the numerous spinal anesthesia procedures caused severe nerve damage. I began researching anything and everything to do with cleft palates and came upon several foundations. I had been reassured by the team at University of Michigan that I had not caused the cleft, and since the genetic testing came back clear, we would probably never know for certain why it had happened. Speculation was that when I lost the other baby, it affected the blood flow to Connor, causing the mouth to not properly grow. In layman's terms, it was a fluke. Connor's surgeries were all successful, even though the emotional ordeal of handing my son over, time and again, and having to trust a medical team to hand him back to me healthy was trying. The demon named "Why Me?" began to fade, and I decided to reopen my intuition and use the lessons I had learned in helping others.

My marriage continued to deteriorate, with my husband's temper becoming even more volatile as his unhappiness escalated. My depression didn't help create a good foundation, but his insensitivity also wasn't healing the relationship. I begged him to go to couples counseling, but his therapy was punching the walls anytime he was upset with me or aggravated at my accusations.

As a child, I always had a pen and notebook in hand, writing either poetry or short stories. As I grew older, I continued my writing and sold several stories to magazines and research papers and educational publications. It was my escape from the world.

At the end of 1997, I came upon the Professional Association of Santa's Elves (PASE) and began Sent by Santa, writing personalized Santa letters. Soon afterward, I was elected to the Board of Elves. My letters were different because each letter was written using my intuition and psychic gift. Obviously, those who were ordering the letters didn't have a clue. I based my letters on information that the parent or grandparent gave me, but I always included extra information. I wrote every letter in a positive tone without blackmailing children to eat all their peas in exchange for a visit from Santa. Instead, it was a pat on the back, reassuring them that they were loved and watched over. My business grew from just a few to thousands a season. I didn't start the project as a "get rich quick" scheme; it was merely my way of sharing my gift and helping out some of the cleft charities.

The writing business helped to reclaim my independence while reopening my intuition, which had felt so evil and wrong before. Although I had always worked outside of the home and had a college education, I knew in the back of my head that one day I would be on my own with the kids, and I had to be prepared. It was just a matter of the timing. The knuckle marks in the drywall were beginning to happen all too frequently.

## eleven

# Letting the Light In

He was leaving us, and I was devastated. Months before the confession I knew something was going on, but I only had strange signs as evidence. The man who I had vowed to be with forever, my high school sweetheart, the man with whom I shared two children, was leaving me for another woman— a married woman who was close to the family. I should've trusted the signs that spirit was offering. My guides provided plenty of signs and signals to prepare me about my crumbling marriage, but I not only ignored them, I hid from them. One sign came in the form of a rash around my wedding ring. The infection became so bad that I had to remove my ring. I joked, asking if it was perhaps *someone* telling me *something*, but my husband thought I was being overly dramatic *again*. An excuse was offered that I was probably becoming allergic to jewelry. Oddly, though, I could wear jewelry on any other part of my body. It wouldn't be until the last clue that I finally asked. And he told.

We had made it a tradition to have a pool party every Fourth of July weekend. Our friends would come in from all over. During the daytime we would barbecue, swim, and play volleyball and bocce ball. At night, we would have a huge bonfire and just talk. Most of our friends would stay the night, and we would have a pancake breakfast in the morning. However, at the end of June 1997, the year Connor was born, our home was ravaged by a tornado. Although the foundation of the home stood solid, we lost most of our roof, the chimney, and several trees. We also were without power for over a week. I contemplated just canceling the party, but my husband didn't think it would be a problem—after all, we were going to be barbecuing and outside. As our friends showed up, the workers came to restore the power, which I felt relieved for, but I still had a sense of uneasiness that I couldn't quite put my finger on.

I could see the way that he looked at her that day and knew then why he didn't want to cancel the festivities. When in the middle of the night Alto told me that I needed to see something, I got up and followed him into the basement, where I saw my husband of eight years and a family friend locked in an embrace. They didn't know that I had caught them, so I merely backed up to the stairway and cleared my throat before walking back into the room. Their faces said it all, but I didn't let on that I knew. The timing wasn't quite right.

Every single time we got together with a group of friends, not only did I break out with the rash around my wedding band, but storms would brew. Not small storms—awful storms that held tornadoes. It became a joke that I controlled the weather with my anger; however, I knew it was symbolism, running much deeper than a dark cloud in the sky, that said storms were brewing in my own marriage.

An October evening, three months after our party, several of our friends met for dinner at a local restaurant. I carefully watched the interaction between my husband and our friends and saw that look again; it was much more than just a friendly glance. As we went to our separate cars, I looked up at the harvest moon lighting my world with clarity and the need for uncovered secrets. Hours later, my world would come crashing down around me. I thought that the confession would break me, and it almost did. My soul, spirit, heart, and faith were ripped into millions of pieces as my naïve happily-ever-after wishes were like fine dust drifting in the wind. Begging, pleading, crying, and begging more only made him more certain that leaving was the right thing. Heck, I wouldn't have wanted to stay with me either.

My initial reaction to the infidelity was to run, and I ran to a friend's home. We were neighbors and our daughters were also friends. As I cried to her about how dumb I was and how sad I was, she told me that she, too, had an affair—an affair with my husband! I raced back home, feeling as if I had been slapped twice. I just wanted the truth and my intuition was so numb that I couldn't tell what the truth was.

"Did you have an affair with Jayme, too?" I screamed.

"Absolutely not! She's nuts!"

I didn't know what to believe. All I knew was that he was leaving. I wish that I could say that the signs and my intuition helped prepare me for the divorce, but they didn't. It still hurt just as badly, and if anything, it made me feel stupid. Stupid that I didn't follow through when the first red flag appeared rather than opting to ignore it and hope that it was all my imagination.

The challenge of being a single mom, looking for a job that would help me pay the bills, and taking care of a large, old house overwhelmed me. On top of that, the spirits decided to continuously pester me like a two-year-old pulling on my apron strings. But what really got me was that one of the spirits was none other than my soon-to-be-ex's grandmother. Night after night I would wake up to what I thought was one of the kids crying, but when I checked I would find them peacefully asleep. However, I'd also see the empty rocking chair rocking away in the living room. I could make out the shadow of an older lady, head bowed and mourning. Several weeks later, exhausted from lack of sleep and stress, I finally yelled that she had to stop haunting me and go and bother her grandson instead. Suddenly, the stereo came on, blasting "Angry Man" by Styx. At that moment I felt I was going crazy and perhaps needed to talk to a minister.

Even though I was afraid the minister of our church would throw holy water on me or call someone to put me in a straitjacket, I made an appointment for early afternoon, dropped Micaela off at preschool, and asked a friend to watch Connor. I waited in the church office, afraid that perhaps someone who knew me would see me. Church, although it teaches that gossip is a sin, tends to be hypocritical and filled with parishioners talking about who missed church, who has who in church with them, and who is cheating on whom. It's just human nature, I suppose, but disheartening all the same. The distinguished-looking minister with warm eyes came out of his office, grabbed my hand, and gently guided me to a seat.

His office was packed with books and paperwork, and adorned with hundreds of cards and gifts from grateful parishioners. This was the man we had sought out when getting married, so I was embarrassed to be talking to him about the end of our union. As I sat down across from him, the minister's eyes looked into mine with wonder. In high school, I was the good girl: an A/B student, active in youth group, the choir, the band, drama, varsity sports—an all-American girl. The reason I was sitting across from him wringing my hands profoundly confused him.

I was raw, yet deeply numb, and I told him everything. I elaborated on my husband's infidelity, and then blurted out, "I see ghosts. I see angels. I see spirits. And they talk to me!" My minister looked at me blankly and asked me to further explain the degree of communication. At that moment, a family member of his came through. A son I never knew he even had. Tears shone in his eyes and he hugged me, giving me his blessing to pursue the work he believed

I was given by God. It sounds so simple, but a theology debate with me playing the devil's advocate took place over a matter of a few hours, with questions like "How do you know I am not talking to something evil and dark?" "How can I tell the difference?" and "If I am of the light, why does the church call this wrong?" Some questions couldn't be answered or had to be mulled over by both of us.

I continued to consult with him for several months and he counseled me. I told him what heaven, the Other Side, was like according to those who had crossed over. He told me that it couldn't be easy being who I was, but that if it were easy, everybody would do it. He also cautioned me about the types of people who would try to play theology *Jeopardy* and ridicule me.

"Maybe you should see a medium," he suggested to me one afternoon.

I was stunned that he could even offer such a thing. I simply shook my head and told him that I would think about it. I did, but after looking at advertisements and searching the Internet for area mediums, most looked like the stereotypical types: cape, wand, mystical, and magical, which, to me, equated to a joke.

Despite the stirring of positive changes within me, keeping my marriage intact was hopeless. My husband decided that he was not going to give up his significant other, so I could either deal with that or file for divorce. I did the latter. It was one of my most painful moments ever. While looking over the papers at my attorney's office, I sobbed shamelessly.

I was about to sign my marriage away when my attorney pulled the paperwork away. "Make sure that you are ready, Kristy," he said. "Are you really ready?" I knew that there was no other alternative. There could be no more begging and no more sacrificing. I felt my grandfather's presence standing next to me, his hand on my shoulder, in comfort. I looked up at his spirit. He looked melancholy, and I worried that maybe he thought I hadn't tried enough. Maybe if I had lost weight. Maybe... there were just so many maybes. My grandpa whispered, "I will always stand by your side, Kristy. You do what you know you have to do." And I signed the papers with tears still streaming down my face.

# twelve

# The Magnolia Tree

It was a mild March afternoon when I decided some fresh air would do us all good. It had been a rough few months since the awful divorce, and the fog around my soul was still slowly lifting. Stretching, I sat down on the whitewashed wooden lawn chair near my garden and admired the magnolia tree in full bloom. A butterfly fluttered into my daughter Micaela's hair. She let out a delighted squeal. Connor, only a month shy of his third birthday, grabbed his bug net in a gallant attempt to catch it. The butterfly's wings glimmered in the sunlight, giving the illusion of a fairy. With a sprite's mischief, the butterfly danced around both kids, teasing. Flying back over to the garden, the butterfly took a final taste of my bright yellow yarrow and flew away. How symbolic that simple moment would later become.

The divorce had been long and painful, and I admit that I sank into a deep depression. My friends and family helped out with the kids as I brooded in self-pity. I had equated my marriage to life itself; it had been my everything. I couldn't imagine going on without him because, without him, we weren't a family. Or so I thought at the time. My heart stung from sorrow, and I felt as if my soul had quickly been replaced with darkness.

Micaela glanced up at me with her soft blue eyes, bent down in the grass to pick up something, and ran over to me. She gently placed a soft pink magnolia flower on my lap, offered me a kiss on the cheek, and ran back to look for butterflies.

Planted several decades ago by the kids' great-grandparents, the old magnolia tree was something magical. Just the sight of the tree made me smile—even on my darkest days. I waited through many long winters for the first bloom to appear and told the kids that the blooms on the crooked old magnolia tree were sure signs that spring was approaching. Spring—a time for rebirth. That innocent gesture from a fair-faced five-year-old awakened me from my melancholy.

I honestly believed that my life was over and that I would never love again or at least never experience joy. What I didn't realize was that it was only a time of metamorphoses as my wings dried in order for me to fly again. It may feel as if our wings have been cut, but in essence we only have to believe that they will regrow in order for us to fly again.

That year the old magnolia tree bloomed twice, once in March and again in October. The neighbor across the street had called me to tell me to look at the tree as another harvest moon began to rise. On the top branches were dozens of pink flowers, giving me the message that I, too, would bloom again.

My anger at the universe began to slowly fade. During the divorce I had lost my job, and although I was devastated at the time and felt that once again the world was out to get me, I quickly received a new job as an operations manager. Most of my new coworkers were younger than me, but they helped me take my mind off my problems. They invited me out after work and introduced me to new people who liked me for who I was. And I slowly began to BELIEVE in myself and in other people again.

# thirteen

# An Angel

I was facing the second Christmas without my husband, the kids' dad, and it felt like ice picks in my heart. That year, I had taken a lot of time off to try to figure out who I was and what I wanted out of life, but I still felt lost, as if everybody, including my guides, had abandoned me.

"We went over this last night at your home, Mom. The ex…" A sob caught in my throat as I talked to my mom on the phone. The reality was still settling in that it was technically my first Christmas as a single mom. My husband, er, ex-husband, had left two weeks before Christmas the previous year and the divorce had been signed near what would've been our ninth wedding anniversary, just a week before the holiday. Anytime "Blue Christmas" came on, I wanted to throw a pillow at the radio. The last year had been a cloud of depression, sadness, and the blues. If it hadn't been for the kids, I didn't know what I would've done. But I knew I had to still keep going—even if it felt like I was merely going through the motions.

"The ex is coming to pick up the kids shortly and I am going to crawl into the PJs and fuzzy socks Dad and you gave me, and hang out on the couch and watch some movies. I'm really okay, Mom." I wasn't sure if I really was, or if I was just trying to convince myself of it.

My mind went back to the time when their father took them for their first overnight—away from me, away from home. He smiled at me, mouthed "thank you," and walked out the door with two little ones on either side of him. I crumbled, thankful that the refrigerator held me up as I sobbed for what felt like an eternity. I still hadn't gotten used to the idea of being without the kids. The house was much too quiet and my thoughts much too loud.

I could hear Mom take a long draw on a cigarette—a huge indication that she was extremely stressed, and I hurt knowing that I was the cause. I also knew that if I went over to their home, my parents' disappointment/anger/sadness/bitterness (pick an emotion) would only accentuate my own disappointment/anger/sadness/bitterness. It wouldn't be pretty.

"Okay. But if you change your mind, we have lots of food left over from last night. At least you could come over and make a plate."

"Maybe, Mom. I might just come with the kids tomorrow. Love you." The tears started again, but I choked the goodbye out and hung up.

As I put the phone back on the cradle, the doorbell rang. Micaela squealed and ran for the door, fully expecting it to be her father. But standing there instead was a man wearing a UPS uniform and holding a large box. "Just sign here," he instructed. "Merry Christmas!"

"Merry Christmas," I responded, dragging the box inside.

Confused, I looked to make sure it was my name. It was. With the kids gathered around, I opened the box to discover several wrapped presents inside addressed to the kids, with the "From" noted as Santa.

"Who are they from, Mommy?" my daughter inquired.

"Santa must've forgotten some things," I said, still stunned as I took everything out of the box looking for a card or any indication of who had sent it, but there was nothing.

"Wait, mommy, this one has your name on it." My daughter handed me a box, but instead of the "From" being Santa Claus, it said "An Angel."

"Can we open them?"

"Yeah, sure."

I watched as they tore into the gift wrap: a doll, a dollhouse, and clothes for Micaela, and a truck, clothes, and bath toys for Connor.

"Open yours!" they urged.

Inside was a beautiful card that simply read:

*I know you've had a tough year, but I wanted to show you that your angels are still around you, even if you don't feel them.*
*Christmas Angel*

In the box was a candle, shampoo, and soap; a gift certificate to a restaurant and another to a grocery store; and a scarf. Attached to the scarf was another note that read:

*Wrap a scarf around you when you feel lost. Feel the warmth that it gives you and remember that your angels wrap their wings around you daily.*

The tears flowed. It had nothing to do with the presents, but everything to do with having felt abandoned.

I didn't know who the Christmas angel was, but whoever it was gave me more than just gifts that year.

After that first Christmas, I started to feel more settled. I could make whatever I wanted for dinner without my husband criticizing. If the potatoes were lukewarm, I didn't have to hear about it. If he was testy, I wouldn't have to worry about knuckle marks in the drywall. Until life was just me and the kids, I never realized that my husband put me on edge. And I started to realize that the rose-colored glasses were clearly tinted with a faux finish. It didn't take away the fact that I had loved him and we had two beautiful children, but I started to feel calmer. I had never lived alone, but my guides began to show up more and more and my confidence grew.

# fourteen

# A New York Minute

Every one of us has our own light that shines, but over time that light can begin to dim and we lose ourselves. Oftentimes, we are the main culprit and cover our own light because we are afraid to shine. And then sometimes we allow others to dim the light, which can happen in a love relationship or business partnership.

We carry so much *stuff* around with us that shadows the light within. Unfortunately, people often choose a love relationship, or even a job, in an effort to feel secure, only to realize that choice was born of fear. Then, as time continues, disappointment grows and dims the light within.

After my divorce, I feared not having stability. How was I supposed to deal with two small kids? I became hungry to find a replacement "father" for the kids and a husband to take care of me, so I became "The Date Queen." Through the divorce, I had lost all my baby weight and kept my girly curves, so I looked healthy and attracted men's attention. I wasn't intimate with these men, but found myself going out on more than my share of dates.

I tried to go about it the right way and went to a divorce-recovery class at a local church (the same place my dad had taken me years back to listen to the exorcist). The church, the size of a mall, was filled with hundreds of folks who were newly divorced or going through a divorce. I was in awe at all of the hurt people. Talk about energy overload! We were placed in random groups and had to come up with a name for our group. All of us were the types who weren't thrilled with authority or rules, so our group leader labeled us "The Mavericks," and the name stuck. The minister was quite aware of the hurt and the need for bandages, so he had a rule forbidding us to date anybody in that room. In fact, he told us not to date anybody for at least a year. It sounded like torture. I did follow his rule about not dating within the group, but by the end of graduation (yes, we had a divorce graduation!), I would say 80 percent were dating one another.

My friends and coworkers, however, were setting me up on date after date, and I went, mostly for conversation and companionship. Also, I was pretty poor and enjoyed the free dinners! None of the dates really clicked. I was still grieving the loss of my fairy tale. But then one date frightened me to just stop.

He was a former Navy Seal who had taken a liking to me. I liked the idea of being taken care of, and he liked the idea of taking care of someone. We talked on the phone for a few weeks before going out on an official date. The ex had the kids for the weekend, so I thought it beat sitting and watching old movies while sniffling over my ice cream. The former Seal picked me up and offered me a hug, and I instantly got a jolt of electricity. Not the good kind. The small talk on the way to the restaurant was awkward and I started regretting not settling in with Julia Roberts instead. He let me off at the restaurant door while he parked the car. I went in and offered the reservation name, which was met by wide eyes from the hostess.

"I hope you don't find this pushy," she said, "but have you known this guy long?"

Talk about red flags! "No, this is our first date," I told her.

"Okay, well, we need to come up with an emergency plan to get you out of here!"

It seemed he went all out with rose petals around the table and ordered a violinist—he even had jewelry for me. Not a ring, but a bracelet. The hostess interrupted us in the middle of dinner with a made-up emergency call and a waiting taxi. That night, and for five nights afterwards, he sat outside my house, watching. I told him I didn't feel a connection with him, but he refused to accept my wishes. Eventually, the police had to be called as he would sit outside of my house, night after night, all night. It was then that I decided I needed to take a safer route by not dating altogether. It didn't last long.

I had previously been introduced to Jason by friends. He had just moved from Georgia to Michigan and was still settling in when we started exchanging emails and phone calls. He was a great listener and, although his communication style was more assertive and blunt than mine, he gave me a new perspective on life. He was intellectually engaging and very charming. He lived about an hour away from me, but came over on the weekends to help me with all of my overwhelming house projects or just go out to lunch or shopping. He was good company and he was great with the kids. We quickly fell into a relationship pattern and before I knew it, I was on a plane to New York to meet his family, and instantly fell in love with them.

I attempted to explain my psychic abilities, but as an engineer, he had the usual black-and-white logic, so I found myself once again stuffing it down, afraid of ruining what I felt was blossoming.

The relationship felt like a whirlwind, and my work friends tried to slow me down. Even my ex-husband mentioned several times that he thought I was making a huge mistake, as it was too soon, going too fast, and I wasn't thinking straight. "Well, I'll show him," I thought. He didn't think I would find anybody and had even said that to me before he left me. I was going to prove to him that I could find someone, but what about the happiness factor?

Jason convinced me to purchase and move into a smaller house just a few miles away from the old marital home. "You need new beginnings," he would tell me time and time again. The new home was cute and I was excited, but unfortunately my children were starting to resent me for all of the changes. Then, just a few months after the move, with a puppy with a ring tied to the bow, Jason asked me to marry him. I said yes. A call to his parents was met with instant wedding plans in progress that felt completely out of control. A date was circled on the calendar, colors were chosen, and his family would plan and pay for it all—as long as it was in New York. My parents didn't take the news quite as positively. They weren't fans of my choice (or the timing) and repeatedly asked me to reconsider. All the while I responded, "But he's good to me and the kids…" And he was.

However, we saw one another every other weekend. It wasn't a relationship fostered in the real world. My new house that I had just moved into went up for sale, and we began to search for a home that was closer to his work, which would mean that the kids had to switch schools. Connor would be going into first grade and Micaela fourth grade. A large house in the country was selected and the fight began between the ex-husband and me. Over his "dead body" would he allow me to switch the kids' school or allow me to move them so far away, although it was just a forty-five-minute drive. It became a very expensive court battle that resulted in a court-ordered truce. I wouldn't collect child support and the kids would go to a mutually selected school halfway between his house and our new one. Jason was absolutely irate at the agreement and made it loudly known. He couldn't understand why the kids couldn't go to the public school, and why I couldn't collect my child support. I didn't like arguing; the court expenses were becoming more than the child support, so I compromised. Jason felt as if I'd sold my soul, and I was angry and upset that he couldn't understand my predicament. I could literally see the red flags.

The next sign came in the form of the flu. We weren't married yet, but Jason had signed on the dotted lines for the home. I picked up the kids from school only for Connor to vomit everywhere halfway to the new house. Should I go back to our home, which was mostly empty, or the new home, which was mostly empty? It was at that moment that I felt like I lost everything. The weekend consisted of the four of us lying on the family room floor with trash cans next to us. Not quite the right energy that I wanted to bring into the experience.

Another bit of foreshadowing, another sign, that my guides attempted to offer me, and once again I turned my head away.

# fifteen

## The Bandages

I was showered and sitting in my pink satin robe staring out at the New York State country field. The night at the B&B was less than relaxing as my mind weighed heavily on the upcoming wedding. I had the entire inn to myself. It was a cheerful yellow building that had been a carriage house in the early 1800s and overlooked the mountains and fields where an array of animals made their home. Next to the inn was a forgotten cemetery where the night before, after the wedding rehearsal, I had wandered over. It was as if I needed to talk to those who hadn't given me their opinions yet, a neutral party. Lord knew that every breathing person around me had shared theirs, and my mind was a jumble.

I sat on a fallen log in the darkness and felt a peace wash over me. The shadows began taking form, and I saw my grandpa and my guides: Alto and Tallie. As soon as I saw their presence, I began to sniffle, which turned into deep sobs. I knew I was making a huge mistake marrying this man, but I didn't know how to get out of it. I felt stuck. Their answer for me was that I wasn't—I just had to remove the bandages and leave. I don't like conflict or confrontation, so even though it sounded like a very easy action, how was I supposed to tell more than two hundred people that I was going back to Michigan and that there wasn't going to be a fancy wedding? And where would I go? I had sold my house and the new house was in Jason's name. I would be homeless and out of an awful lot of money. I decided that I would go forward with the wedding and hope that, if anything, I could feel comfortable. I knew I didn't love him and I knew he didn't love me. It was a façade of what we may have both wanted, but really didn't have.

I laughed at the previous day's fiasco. After driving over twelve hours, Jason and I had to go to the courthouse to obtain our marriage license for the next day's ceremony, only I couldn't find my driver's license, a requirement. I took everything out of my purse several times, tore the car apart, and then went through the suitcase. Nothing. I finally had to call my realtor to see if she had a copy that she could fax over to the courthouse, and she did. Problem solved, or so we thought. As we stood in the office of the courthouse, all of the computers malfunctioned and wouldn't turn on. The office worker laughed and asked me if perhaps this was a telling sign. Little did she know that she was hitting very close to the truth. After an hour of the worker playing with the computers, they began to work and the license was printed.

The phone's ring broke my thoughts.

"Hi honey," I heard my mom say on the other line. "Dad's here, too."

"Kristy, are you okay?" he asked.

"Yep, I am just fine." My voice cracked.

"I am going to fly out, Kristy. Or let me wire you money so that you and the kids can fly home." Mom had never flown and for her to offer to get on a plane to be with me set off my emotions.

"No, I'm okay, really." I began to sob.

"Kristy," my dad began in a stern voice, "just cancel the wedding and come home."

"He's a good man. It'll be okay. I have to go; the photographer just showed up!" I lied.

My parents offered me their love and support before we hung up, and all I could do was fling myself on the bed and cry until I heard the stones crush from the photographer's car tires. It was time to paste a smile on my face and get dressed into my lovely ivory lace wedding gown. And like a cruel joke from the universe, putting another spotlight on the fact that I was making a bad choice, the limousine driver we hired to take me to the church didn't show up and the rain started coming down in sheets and didn't stop, which didn't make for a fabulous wedding at a yacht club. The old wives' tale is that if it rains on your wedding you'll cry plenty of tears throughout your marriage. The signs were piling up, but I chose to ignore them to save face. I married Jason.

Back in Michigan at my new home, driving the kids back and forth to school over an hour each way, and coming home late at night to an empty house was not how I thought my life would turn out. At this time, I was working for a public school in the human resources department, and, although I was hired to help promote a warmer environment for employees, I was subjected to a tough boss who didn't much like me, since I was too creative and Pollyanna for his liking. The kicker was that he was the one who hired me. I was sad at work. I was sad on my way to a home that didn't feel anything like a home, and I suspected that my new groom was cheating just a few weeks into the marriage. No, I didn't suspect, I *knew*.

I lay in bed, feeling like a stranger in the house, and asked for my guides to help me. I hadn't felt them for quite some time, and I didn't really blame them. I had abandoned them like an old childhood toy. They tried to get through to me, but I ignored them or pretended that they didn't exist. And now here I was asking for their assistance again. A dark shadow crept across my closet door and I sat straight up in bed.

"Alto?" I called out, hoping that it was him. No answer. "Tallie?" I asked, but again I heard nothing.

The shadow got larger and larger and took over an entire wall of the bedroom and then split into three wisps of smoke that lingered above my footboard, until I finally felt the presence of Alto and Tallie and the negative energy flew out the window. I shook my head to make sure that I wasn't dreaming, but I was wide awake. Alto looked disappointed in me and Tallie's blue eyes shined with tears. What was happening? I wondered, worried. The kids ran into the room, both crying.

"We saw something... it was large and stood over me," Connor tried to explain through gasps.

I couldn't explain it to them, nor did I think I wanted to. I only pulled my blankets back and let them crawl into bed with me. I felt safer with them nearby and I knew that my husband wouldn't be joining me anyhow as his girl-friend was in town, knowledge that didn't require snoop-ing or intuition.

A week before I'd woken up sick and decided to call into work late. As I was taking a shower, the bathroom door wildly swung open and the shower curtain ripped from the hooks.

"Why are you here?" he demanded, his hands on his hips, making his already large frame even larger.

I grabbed the shower curtain and covered myself with it, the water still pouring down on top of me. I was too fright-ened to move, turn the water off, grab a towel, or step out of the shower. His scowl spoke volumes—I had interrupted his plans. I told him that I had woken up ill and was just getting ready to go into work, albeit late, but my excuse didn't make him budge; instead, he accused me of ruining his day. I could feel his temper growing as he swatted at a picture hanging on the wall. It crashed to the floor, shattering. He stormed out. I could hear his heavy footsteps descend the staircase, and then the tears erupted. Once again, I had somehow written myself into yet another soap opera. Carefully, I stepped out of the shower hoping that I didn't cut my foot on the glass, quickly got dressed, and ran downstairs to grab my shoes and keys to leave. A large bouquet of roses in my favorite color of soft peach sat on the table. I could hear giggles, as if mocking me, coming from the basement. I was hurt and angry, but it wasn't for me—it was because now my children were involved. Instead of walking out the front door, I stormed down the basement steps to see his married girlfriend sitting on his lap. They looked at me, grinned at one another, and began to kiss. I couldn't take much more and started screaming and a fight of words ensued. They both chased me upstairs, calling me names, saying that I was an awful person, and tag teaming me with emotional and verbal abuse until I was locked out of the house without shoes or keys, only my cell phone, which I used to dial 911.

The officer was a young man in his thirties. He listened to me with kind eyes and told me to wait while he spoke to the others. Just a few minutes went by, and then he walked me back into the home to gather clothes and toys for the kids, my clothes, and the keys. He instructed my husband and his girlfriend to stay away from the home so as to not cause any domestic dispute. After seeing the mess in the bathroom, he told me that I should go seek help at a women's shelter. I was stunned. I thought I was tough enough, and I didn't need help from anybody else. I thought I could handle it all by myself. My divorce attorney told me that in no way, shape, or form could I move out—even if my life was at stake—and so I asked the kids' father to keep them for longer periods of time, and when I didn't have them I stayed at the local women's shelter, my girlfriend's couch, and, once in a great while, at my mom and dad's house. But during the divorce proceedings, which lasted longer than the entire marriage, I mostly slept in the marital home, with the bedroom door locked and a nightstand up against it for extra protection. I knew that I had Alto and Tallie to help if I needed them.

I was embarrassed to discuss it with my family, friends, or coworkers and kept it under wraps for as long as I could out of pure embarrassment. I mean, I'm a psychic so I should be able to see my future with clarity, right? It isn't so much that I can't see my future, but the fact that I don't particularly want to know my future. I would much rather be guided on to the right path than have my life written out for me. How boring would that be? And, although my guides, family, and friends tried to show me the right path, I was the stubborn one who put the blinders on.

Looking back, that time in my life feels surreal. It was a bandage that I tried to glue on my wounds that still bled for the kids' father. I wanted to prove that I could be happy, but in the end I made everybody miserable. I do, however, believe that everybody we involve ourselves with comes with a lesson. Before that relationship, I hadn't traveled at all, but during it I learned to love to explore, to travel, and to be spontaneous. I also began to trust and listen to my guides and family and friends when they send through a forewarning and not get defensive. Message received.

# sixteen

# *Faithless*

Looking out the second-floor bedroom window onto the lonely street, I begged for answers to nobody in particular—or was it to everybody? A bit of glass-half-empty, glass-half-filled was the table tennis game going on in my head, and it was feeling more like dodgeball and I was losing, emotionally beaten. Even the sun couldn't warm the sadness that surrounded my soul, and it didn't help that the landscape I stared at was just as abandoned as I felt, every single home across the street either left to be burned down or home to someone who had lost everything and ached only to have a roof over their head, even if just for one night.

I was always so good at giving people advice at work, so much that I had gotten a great job working in the human resources department where my office was constantly busy with employees seeking advice. I also was still writing my Santa letters that helped kids (and adults) believe in themselves. And yet I had so much melancholy, but was it around me? Or within me? How was I supposed to give hope and support to my employees and the kids when I myself felt hopeless? I despised hypocrites and the last thing that I wanted was to be one. My cell phone chimed just as I was about to tear into another round of emotional dodgeball.

"It's over," I said numbly. There was no need to fake a cheery greeting to a best friend.

"Which is why we are cel-e-brating!" Kay sang. "I'll be picking you up in ten minutes, so change out of your fuzzy PJ bottoms and that ugly concert shirt and, for cripes sakes, Kristy, put some makeup on."

"Whaaa…" I tried replying, but realized she hung up. I rolled my eyes at the receiver, wishing that I could just spend the rest of the day, night, and maybe the next lifetime of days and nights in my own cloud of despair. It was starting to feel comfortable. Okay, probably not. And just to make it clear, I was wearing yoga pants, not fuzzy PJ bottoms.

Life was funny, not in a ha-ha way, but in a philosophical *hmmm* kind of way. Nobody likes change, especially a drastic change such as a breakup, divorce, loss of job, or loss of loved one. It could be the worst partner or the worst job, but knowing that you are waking up next to someone or heading to a job, any job, can sometimes be a comfort, until you are forced into a different route and realize that maybe it wasn't good after all.

I realized through my own trials and tribulations that I had lost my dream and I had lost faith. I had given up on a college scholarship, forgotten how to feel pretty, and lost the love that I had for myself. I was only half of the person that I had been and less than half of the person that I wanted to be. My dreams had to change due to life circumstances, and when life threw a curveball, they had to change again, but that didn't mean that I had to sacrifice or even postpone them. Yet I did. Life changes continue to occur, but figuring out ways to get through them and grow is the biggest test. I've found that setting goals, being grateful for what I have and what I believe I'm worthy of receiving, and taking action helps me stay positive even during the toughest times. Sure, there were many times that I wanted to put on those fuzzy PJ bottoms and beat myself up—we all have those days—but even the fuzzy PJs can't soften the emotional bruises. Releasing the old habits that anchor you to the past gives you the power to move forward to live in the now and set goals for the future.

"You know what you should do?" Kay asked, munching on a chocolate-chip cookie. Kay knew me better than I knew myself on most days, and even though she told me to get dressed up, she took me to my favorite place—a bookstore.

"Run away from home?" I replied, pouring more sugar into my vanilla latte.

Kay grabbed the sugar container and set it on the table next to us, like a mother scolding a child. "No, you should go see a psychic."

I answered with a roll of the eyes. "Really? For a psychic to tell me that my life sucks and the future looks even dimmer. No thank you."

"So cynical. Where is my positive Kristy?"

The conversation quickly changed to who I was predicting to be voted off *Survivor*, but I couldn't stop thinking that maybe Kay was right. I had lost my faith. Faith isn't easy to have when it keeps getting squished, but it lightens the darkened paths by bringing you sunbeams from heaven. We each create our individual time of transformation by taking charge of the creations and releasing the shackles from the spirit and soul. I was about to find the flame to light my lanterns.

# seventeen

# True Self

I was lost. I was twice divorced, not even thirty years old, and wandering on an empty, lonely path. Kay's words that I should see a psychic kept going through my head. Even though I knew I had abilities, I was extremely skeptical of others. Still, something told me to do it, so I made the appointment on a Tuesday for Saturday morning. Each day I thought about canceling the appointment, but didn't. I even drove to the center that Saturday morning and pulled in, then pulled out. I drove around and pulled back in.

Iinitially, I wasn't sure what drew me to the metaphysical shop. Okay, that was a lie. Deep down I did know, but saying it made me want to choke. It was pure desperation. I had passed the metaphysical shop numerous times, as it was just minutes from my home, but on that dull gray November day, it was as if a magnet were pulling me in.

Parking as far from the storefront as possible, I glanced around before exiting the safe haven of my car, afraid that someone I knew might see me. My hands shook as I opened the entrance door. Wind chimes jingled and as I stepped inside, I was taken aback by the smell of incense. I was greeted by a black cat who sat straight up on the counter as if awaiting my arrival. Its harvest moon–colored eyes met mine, and he stretched out his front paws and sprawled out on the glass. A smooth and friendly male voice called from a storeroom in the back, "Be right there."

Glancing around the store, I didn't see any voodoo dolls or satanic-looking items. That was a relief. Having absolutely no idea what to expect, I had pictured crystal balls, pentagrams, hundreds of lit candles, and a chanting coven. Instead I saw a well-lit room displaying different types of stones, crystals, and jewelry. On one shelf were several books from well-known psychics such as Sylvia Browne and John Edward, all sharing their own stories or giving suggestions on how to build one's intuition. On another shelf sat a large display of tarot card decks. The bright cards looked friendly and not as sinister as my imagination had drawn from movies and television shows. The butterflies in my stomach slowly began to settle down.

"Sorry about that," a man said as he walked quickly to the counter. "What can I help you with?"

Our eyes met and he smiled. He didn't look like a psychic, or at least what I believed a psychic would look like. He appeared to be in his late fifties, about six-foot-one, and was wearing blue jeans and a black polo shirt with the store's name and a picture of a moon imprinted upon it. It seemed all of my initial impressions were amiss.

"I'm not sure," I said a bit shyly. "A reading?"

"Have you ever had a reading before?" he said, leading me to the back of the store.

"No, I haven't. In fact I'm so nervous right now that I feel like I'm being taken to the gas chamber!" I confessed with a quick laugh.

"Don't worry," he reassured me, as he opened the door to a small office. "We will be gentle."

We? Puzzled, I gazed around, but only saw the two of us. Well, not including the cat, but I decided to keep quiet and sat in the chair that he pulled out for me. The room was decorated in a soothing aloe green with bright white trim. The walls displayed pictures of what I assumed to be family and friends, along with several drawings of angels.

"My name is Josh," he said, sitting down across a round table from me.

On the table sat a tape recorder, tapes, and several different stones. One looked like a rose quartz, one was an amethyst, and another stone was flat and brown. Josh grabbed a tape, wrote the date on it—November 8—and put it into the player and hit Record. He grabbed the murky brown stone and began stroking it between his index finger and thumb. His hands looked worn from years of hard physical work.

"I'm a psychic medium," he began. "I connect with the world of Spirit and tune into your energy. The messages I receive for you come directly from Spirit. We all have free choice, which means that what I tell you today doesn't necessarily mean that it will happen. *You* have choice to change the path. Understand?"

I nodded silently.

"First thing I need you to do is to tell me your full name, and then take a deep breath in and breathe out."

"Kristy Sue." I hesitated, thinking what last name to use. The divorce had muddled up my mind. I felt like I lacked an identity. I finally decided upon my maiden name. "Schiller. Kristy Sue Schiller," I firmly stated, and, as instructed, breathed in deeply through my nose and out through my mouth.

The psychic closed his eyes for a few seconds and began. "The first thing I see is…"

He quickly opened his eyes and looked long and hard at me, saying nothing. My heart felt as if it stopped and the feeling of wanting to bolt boiled within me, but doing that would have been rude, so I waited.

"Kristy, do you see things? I mean… do you see spirits? Angels? Do strange things happen to you? Lights flashing on and off? Pictures falling? Shadows from the corner of your eye?"

And so it was finally brought to light by an expert, along with his spirit guides and my own guides talking together, that I, too, was psychic… or a spiritual intuitive as I honestly prefer to call it.

It was a relief to finally put a name to it. I knew that I was different. I had always been able to read people's emotions and body language and was often awakened at night by unexplained things: loud noises, whispers, shadows, and cold air. The phone would ring and I would know who was calling even before they said anything. I knew when there would be snow days before the weatherman called it, and I baffled classmates and teachers for knowing when a pop quiz would happen.

Since I was a small child, I was drawn to cemeteries, where I would wander around gravestones until I found one I liked. Then I'd sit down and have a conversation in my head. I had no idea that those conversations were actually with the spirits of the deceased. I laughed at the thought. I always thought I was just talking to myself. I wasn't quite certain which was crazier.

Many times I felt guilty for seeing spirits. Was *I* evil? I wasn't even allowed to look at my horoscope in the Sunday newspaper without censure, so trying to explain to my parents that I not only saw, but also spoke to, their dead parents was taboo. I was certain *that* wasn't going to be accepted very well.

Before ending the session, Josh asked me if I was interested in a job. A job doing readings? I wondered. I had a job, but with the divorce and lack of money, another paycheck would come in handy. I decided to hold off on giving him an answer, but I was quite tempted. I had never formally read for anybody, but it was an intriguing idea.

That cold November day changed my life. The real reason that I went to get a reading was because on that date, my second divorce had become final and I felt lost. The reassurance that there was something better to come was calling out to me a bit more strongly than the full bottle of Valium on my nightstand. I was seeking guidance because it seemed nobody else could offer that to me. I wanted a light at the end of the tunnel, and hoped it wasn't a train waiting to meet me head-on. I received more guidance than I could've imagined by finally admitting to myself who and what I was.

After my session, I drove back to Jason's house where the kids and I were still living. I hadn't any clue how we were going to move out. I lost thousands of dollars during those few months of marriage and depleted my retirement fund to pay someone to take my house off of my hands. I was homeless and living with an incredibly abusive and sick individual who wanted me to suffer for whatever reason his bipolar mind had concocted. The kids and I were still sleeping in one bedroom, with the door locked and heavy furniture in front of it. It was the safest haven I could come up with except for the few times I had to escape to a friend's couch or to the women's shelter. I was told that if I left the marital house, I would lose everything.

I was getting more and more physically sick until one day I went to the doctor, who diagnosed me with pancreatitis and ordered my gallbladder to be removed immediately. Jason came to the hospital after being missing on some excursion for a week and promised to never leave me again, but I knew it was another falsehood; the divorce papers were already drawn up (after the mandatory waiting period) for our final signatures. As I recovered, I came up with a plan to begin a healthier life. So I called my realtor friend and asked her to set me up with a rental. I didn't care where—I just needed out. And I signed up for a community theater audition. It was time to find my true self, so I needed to immerse myself in what I loved doing. I loved the kids. I loved theater, and we needed a happy and safe environment. I put actions into motion and finally felt the negativity of not just that marriage, but the first marriage gradually start to drip off of me.

That Monday evening I showed up, with Micaela in tow, at the local theater to audition for *The Man Who Came to Dinner.* I had checked out the script and had done my research. I was a nervous wreck and twice walked out the door and back to my car. I was given a number—13, my lucky number—and had my photograph taken and was herded into the seats to await my turn. They were cold readings, and even though I had read the script, it did little to quell my nerves. I chatted a bit with the other actors and began to be even more intimidated as they shared their experiences in LA, Chicago, and New York. They all had professional pictures with them, along with their résumés, some of which listed local commercials and brief walk-ons for shows like *Friends, CSI,* and *House.* All I had was a Polaroid, and the last production I was in was in 1988.

I was finally called up ("Kristy…come on down") to read. Nervous, but excited, as the director handed me the script, I stood in the center of the room, took a deep breath in and out, quickly closed my eyes, and wished for my spirit guides to be with me. Then I opened my eyes and went straight into character. I felt comfortable with my performance, but most of all I was proud that I took the chance. I was shaking so badly and trying not to show it, but after I was done, the audience actually stood up and clapped for me. I think I blushed five shades of red. Micaela also tried out for a singing part. Her overdramatic Leo ways have loved the stage since before she was even three years old.

I was sitting next to a lady who asked me what part I really wanted, and I told her that I hadn't acted in quite a while and wasn't being picky. I just wanted to do something I loved and missed doing. She nodded. After reading a part for the third time, I sat down, and she lovingly patted me on the shoulder and said I was doing great. I asked her what she was trying out for since I hadn't seen her being called up, and she said, "Oh no, dear, I'm the vice president on the board and helping choose the participants." The next day, right as I went to punch out at work, my cell phone rang with the news from the director that I had indeed won myself the part of June Stanley and Micaela received a part in the chorus. My smile followed me home to pack boxes for the move that weekend. New beginnings were ahead of me and I couldn't have been more excited.

# eighteen

# Reset Button

Our new temporary home was a six-hundred-square-foot, two-bedroom duplex that had been built during the World War II era to help house soldiers when they came home. The entire house was about the same size as the bedroom of my previous home. It felt humiliating to move from the upper-class country home into what was called "Shack Town," but I would take the worries of crack houses and guns over the abuse I had experienced any day. At any rate, it was only temporary until I found and closed on a home. In the meantime, I kept busy with play practice and activities with the kids, and I finally made that phone call to Josh, the owner of the local metaphysical center, and accepted a part-time position doing readings.

The kids and I pulled up in front of the store at eight-thirty in the morning the Saturday after moving back to the old side of town. I let out a sigh of relief when I realized I wouldn't need to parallel park. Since the road was virtually empty of vehicles, I pulled right into a spot.

The bells jingled as the three of us made our way into the shop. Josh, who was standing at the front counter, broke into a wide smile as soon as he saw me and I instantly felt at ease.

"I was worried you'd bail on me," he said.

"Me? Would I do a thing like that?" I offered an innocent look.

"The kids can have a seat in the classroom. There's a television and some comfy chairs and couches and I'll show you the fun stuff."

"Maybe this isn't such a good idea, after all," I whimpered pathetically.

He patted my hand. "You'll be fine."

He had more confidence in me than I had in myself.

"So," he asked, "you read tarot cards, right?"

"No," I said, beginning to panic. "I'm, I guess, what they refer to as a medium. I talk to the dead and they give me information."

"Hmm…" Josh bit his bottom lip. At that time there weren't any television shows on that described the differences between a psychic and medium, so I knew he was wondering how he could market me with clients. Grabbing a deck of tarot off the shelf, he handed them to me. "Fake it!"

"Whhaaa…?"

"Not the reading," he said. "Just fake that the information is coming from the cards. People get nervous with you looking at, er, through them."

I nodded, opened the cards, and shuffled. The deck was full of color and characters and they seemed to vibrate in my hands. I could do this. I hoped.

After showing me the inventory of items, the price lists, and how to work the cash register, he led me to the booth where I'd be doing readings. I just prayed there wouldn't be any customers.

No such luck.

Only a few minutes later, a petite lady in her mid-forties came in, her tan screaming that it was as fake as her personality would later prove to be. I hoped she just wanted to buy some stones, or tea, or maybe a book. Nope, she wanted a reading.

I rang her up, after making only two mistakes. I had mad cash register skills from my years of working at Kmart as a teenager. I could scan, ring, and bag at an Olympic pace, but the nervousness of the impending reading was taking over. I led her to the back of the shop and had her sit down across from me. It was a barren little nook, but it held a lot of possibility—and it was mine. I couldn't help but feel excited that I had my own office!

After thirty minutes of hearing the customer whine about her love life or lack thereof, I escorted her out the door with her taped session and my makeshift business card. I was pretty proud of myself. The reading had gone well, though she really didn't seem to want to hear what I had to say. It seemed, instead, she'd just wanted someone to talk to. While her spirit guides had come through loud and clear, she made no effort to listen, thus explaining her lack of a love life. Choosing alcoholics and addicts definitely was not what her guides had wanted for her, but she was so desparate to be loved, she was setting her sights so low that it ensured that would be all she would attract.

I sat down in my chair and pondered the session and immediately felt awful for prejudging her. After all, take away the drugs and alcohol and we had a lot in common. We were both attracting losers, and we were both accepting whatever came along instead of valuing ourselves.

Maybe this wouldn't be bad so bad after all, I thought to myself. Doing readings, that is. I was put in this place for a reason, right?

The past was awful, but it seemed to be granting me the opportunity to change my life and to evolve in a new direction. Happiness would slowly trickle in. When one door closes, another opens, as the saying goes, just like my father had preached to me every time I was having a tough time. This feeling of helping others, of connecting people to the Other Side, felt more powerful and reassuring. No, I hadn't suddenly become all Pollyanna, and I wasn't delusional. I was realistic. I knew that not everyone around me would want to open up, and that was understandable. For every person who didn't believe in me or in this gift, there would be someone else who did and who needed guidance. What is a bittersweet ending without goodbyes and walking away from those things that hadn't been working in my life anyway, I wondered? I had let life disable me. It was a painful truth. I had to say goodbye to people in my life who were keeping me from happiness and truth, and now it seemed that I was being regifted my gift. I didn't feel quite so alone.

The door chimes tinkled once again, snapping me out of deep thought. It was another woman, but this one's energy was much different from the last. My stomach tightened up, and I felt like I was going to vomit right there on top of the incense. This one was going to be a doozy.

"Can I help you?" I asked the woman with the mane of bleached blonde hair, all *Sex and the City* with her hot pink spiked heels and matching purse that I could have sworn I'd seen Paris Hilton don on reruns of *The Simple Life*. She wore a sassy little dress no longer than the T-shirt I wore, minus a bra. She certainly didn't scream natural beauty as much as "*I paid for this; is it working?*" Perhaps I was picking up on her monthly Botox sessions when the first energy I read from her screamed oily snake. I didn't trust her and neither did my guides.

"I heard there was a new girl in town," the stranger said with a condescending smile as she began pawing the merchandise.

I clenched my jaw. A girl? Little Ms. Tawny Kitaen wannabe was calling me a girl?

"I'm Kristy. Can I help you?"

Maybe direct you across the street to Target, so you can buy some clothes that fit! And a bra to boot, I wanted to advise.

She went about the shop, continuing to pick up various things here and there with her freshly manicured red nails. My mom used to warn me about women with red nail polish, and I don't think she would have been too far off with this one. It was obvious she was just being nosy, not really interested in buying anything at all.

"Can I offer you a reading?" I swore in my head and then asked forgiveness. Josh would pay me damned well for this one.

"Oh, Josh is the only one that I ever allow to read for me," she purred.

I'm sure he was. Men are all the same. I sighed in frustration.

She walked back over to the counter and looked at me. "Oh, what the heck. It might be fun."

As fun as another C-section, minus the bundled-up bouncing baby I got in the end, I thought. Taking her money, and noticing the thick wallet, I couldn't help but snicker to myself that I wouldn't have been surprised if she paid me with all singles.

I led her back to the office.

"So what training have you had?" she asked, taking a seat across from me.

"Training?"

"Training as a medium or psychic, or whatever you are."

"I haven't been trained. I was born this way," I said, shrugging my shoulders.

She made a noise that sounded a bit like clucking in the back of her throat.

"Well, I do want my money back if you suck."

"Of course," I said with clenched teeth.

"I love what you did with the space," she said dryly, looking at the bare walls.

"Thanks. It's the new look that everybody is talking about in Manhattan," I said with a smile, trying to look and sound convincing. "I call it ghost white."

The client made another clucking noise and began playing with her purse strap, reminding me of a kitten.

"I need you to close your eyes, take a deep breath in, then release your breath and say your full name out loud."

She did as I instructed.

I took a cleansing breath myself, praying that pure light surrounded me.

My guides flashed images of several men. I mentally begged them not to show me any sexual escapades. "The first thing that the guides are showing me is that you are stringing along several guys at one time."

"Duh, look at me. If you were a man, I'm sure you would want this, too."

I so wanted to vomit on her.

"The first man that they show has the energy of a husband. Or ex-husband. He has ethics and truly had good intentions."

She nodded.

"Then they show another man, which I find odd because I feel a similar energy between him and the first. Wait a minute." I tuned in to the message that I was getting, cocking my head like a dog would, trying to hear clearly. "Are they brothers? No, wait a minute. Are they cousins?"

Her face turned white. "How did you know?" she whispered.

Instead of answering, I continued on as her response validated that I was on the right track. "They show a badge around him. Probably a cop. And then..." I stopped again and looked at her from across the small round table. "You do get around now, don't you?"

She looked nervous.

"Now they show another man. He's older than the others, but I also get a relationship to the other men." Was she getting it on with the entire family? I felt like I was going to need a shower when this was all over. "This one feels dangerous. They show a gun around him also, but I don't believe it has anything to do with serving or protecting to uphold the law."

"Now you're just freaking me out. Josh must have told you this stuff."

"No, Josh didn't tell me anything, I'm a medium, remember?" I was having fun now. Yeah, it was at her expense, but I was starting to feel confident. "Did you want me to continue?"

She hesitated for a moment before answering. "Yes." Then gathering her cockiness, she added, "You owe me my full thirty minutes!"

The time couldn't pass quickly enough.

"They show that you want to get back with your ex, but that he won't have anything to do with it, but you are going to try nonetheless. I don't see it happening. I see another man coming your way soon. Someone who's not even remotely related to the other three. A man much more matched to you."

"Ooooo... What's his name?" She leaned forward, her blue eyes large with excitement. I felt as though I were looking in the eyes of a black widow getting ready to eat her prey.

Sometimes my guides show me names or initials, but I wasn't getting anything. Not even a letter. I did, however, have a description and at that moment I could have kissed my guides.

"Sorry, I don't have a name, but I can tell you what he looks like."

And so the reading continued on without a hitch and thankfully she didn't request her money back. I felt relieved when she finally left, but then just when I thought I could relax, another client came in. One after another they chimed through the doors. It seemed that I was Sideshow Bob, as the rumor mill had spread that there was a new reader in town. Whatever the case, I was making money, and that was good.

# nineteen

# Undercover Psychic

I felt a bit like I was living a double life. I was working in human resources for a fairly traditional and conservative school district, and if they found out that I was working a second job as a medium, I would be forced to choose one or the other. I couldn't tell my parents or the kids' father. He would have my head. So, the kids were sworn to secrecy, and I went on working at the metaphysical center every Thursday evening when the ex had the kids and every Saturday morning with the kids in tow. My life was becoming chaotic, but the busyness was enlightening and welcome. I had also decided to drop my name back into the dating pool, but not to find a longtime companion. Who knew if it was a nudge from my guides or self-mutilation?

In my very first reading, Josh had told me that a few months after the divorce I would meet a man whose first name would begin with the letter "R." He said that the man would have kids, be divorced for some time, and was my soul mate, but to be honest, even though I was dating, I was exhausted and starting to get a bit cynical about re-lationships. I really needed a break, but a few weeks after my psychic appointment, I was asked to go on a blind date.

His name was Chuck and since there wasn't an R in his first name, I thought I was safe. I was embarrassed to tell my mom and dad that I was dating. After the past fiascos, I knew they would disapprove, so instead I asked if they could watch the kids for an hour while I ran errands for the play. They agreed, and I met up with my mystery man at a local restau-rant.

We had previously emailed one another our photos, and I told him what I would be wearing—black pants and a sweater, and he said he would have on jeans and a polo shirt. I can't say that it was love at first sight. Actually, the moment that I saw him it was apparent that he wasn't my type at all and this would probably be our first and last date. He looked a bit like he hadn't stepped out of the 1970s. He was ten years older than me, and looked it, with longish dark brown hair mixed with salt and pepper. I offered him a hug, and although he hugged back, he scowled at me for not wearing what I told him I would be wearing. He was right. It was a warm November, and at the last minute I changed into jeans and a shirt. Instead of being insulted, I laughed at his honesty and wit. We were seated, and before ordering, the jitters of a first date were instantly eliminated and we fell into easy conversation that was comfortable and also felt safe. I hadn't felt safe in years, if I really ever had.

"So what do you do for a living?" Chuck asked me as he stirred his Diet Pepsi with his straw.

I had made a promise to myself to stop disguising who I was. Well, that was half true. I was still keeping secrets from my family. "I work in human resources for Northville Public Schools, but I am a spirit medium."

I checked his expression. He slightly raised his left eyebrow. "And what does being a spirit medium entail?"

"I see, hear, and communicate with those who've crossed over, along with guides and angels," I said with a newfound strength.

"Fascinating. My mom has always been into astrology and that stuff, too."

I nodded. Before I could ask him more, the waitress came with our food.

"Can you pass the ketchup?" Chuck asked me, fixing his burger as I dumped dressing on my salad.

I laughed at the nonchalant attitude. After all, how many dates confessed that they talked to the dead? I went on to tell him of the session that I had with Josh.

"Well, you must not be *the one*," I joked. "He said that my soul mate's name starts with the letter R."

I looked up from my salad to see that he had turned ghost white.

"Does it count that my entire family calls me Robbi and not Chuck?"

Ding, ding, ding.

It was my turn to pale. I decided right then to never offer names to my clients.

Without my realizing it, two hours passed and I had to rush to get back to my parents' house. I knew they would be chomping at the bit. I felt a tad bit like Cinderella at midnight and, as I sped to my car, Chuck stopped me. He opened his car door and pulled out a dozen flowers, a CD, and a stuffed animal and handed them to me.

"You told me your birthday was last week, so this is a bit late, but I thought you might like." He blushed as he piled my arms full of gifts.

I rarely ever got gifts from either husband, and I was grateful. The date had been exhilarating and I was smitten, but played it cool. I gave him another hug.

"Hey, where's my kiss?" he flirted, and kissed me on the lips.

Sparks flew, even though it was a peck.

I couldn't stop thinking about him that night, and before bed I received an email from him that spelled out exactly how I was also feeling. It was love at first sight and there wasn't anything I could do about it.

The next weekend he asked if he could take me out on another date since the kids were with their dad, and I agreed. Though I was humiliated with where I was living, I offered my address.

"Ackley?" he said with a stunned tone to his voice.

Great, he thinks that I am living in the hood and will retract the date.

"I lived on Ackley about fifteen years ago. Wow, I can't believe you live on Ackley!"

The coincidences, or synchronicities as I would much rather consider them, didn't end there. That weekend he went to the basement with me to feed my rabbit, Ginger. I had most of my prized possessions in storage there and one such love was a painting that depicted a little girl standing in the corner, a dog next to her side. Once again he blanched.

"My entire family has that print. My mom has hers hanging in her living room."

Concerts, music, friends, past vacation places, and even our kids' first-name initials were in sync. I had a Micaela and Connor; he had a Molly and Cora. Micaela was born in August, as was Molly. My first marriage and his past marriage ended similarly. We shared the same hurt, the same concerns, and the same dreams. We instantly fell into a comfortable and loving relationship. Although I was incredibly happy and the kids loved Chuck and his girls, many people were unhappy with the situation, including my coworkers, my parents, and my brother. It was just too soon, they would tell me. Or, they would joke about me being Elizabeth Taylor and wondered how many last names I might end up with. I became worried that perhaps I was as blinded as I was with Jason, but this felt better than any other relationship had, and they weren't living it—I was!

We celebrated our first Christmas together and I was absolutely giddy. My mom commented that she had never heard me laugh so much, that even though she couldn't see, she could feel me glowing. But her antennaes were up, and she was worried. Plus, my brother was feeding her all kinds of concerns like Chuck was too old for me or he didn't make enough money. "Chuck Chuck," he would joke whenever he could. I just smirked and bit my tongue.

Our relationship continued to flourish. I purchased a small ranch home, and without me even recognizing it, he slowly began to move in. I was balancing opening night of the play, doing readings at the center, working forty hours at my real job, and being a mom. And then I received the call.

My mom had a heart attack and was placed in the intensive care unit. My brother pulled me aside and again started with the "Chuck Chuck." I burst into tears.

"How dare you prejudge," I yelled and ran out of my mom's room and out of the hospital. I was so exhausted at everybody telling me what to do that my spine was slowly beginning to strengthen. The fight between my brother and me lasted just a day, because that night I received the call that my dad had a heart attack. Rushing to the hospital, I was filled with so much emotion and fear that I might lose both parents. The doctor told us that Dad needed a new stent put in, and he was placed just a few rooms from Mom. She rolled her eyes and said that it was just like him to try to steal her thunder. Although Dad's prognosis was good, Mom's was not. They sent her home anyhow—to await death.

# twenty

# Messenger of Death

The attempted kidnapping back when I was seven years of age had haunted me for more than twenty years, and I had stayed up to date on all the news stories about "The Oakland County killer," who has to this date never been caught.

I was working my dream job (at the time) in the human resources department of a prestigious school district and was sent out to a weeklong conference on safety at Michigan State University in Lansing, Michigan, about an hour away from my home. The long hours and group participation lent to bonding with the other attendees, and we would go out for dinner and just hang out and talk in one another's rooms, studying for the test at the end of the week. One of the participants was a police officer and somehow, I shared with him my story about the spoiled kidnapping attempt, along with my gift of being an intuitive. He worked for a department that was investigating the two-decade-old case, although he was not personally involved. After saying our goodbyes at the end of the week, he took my business card, and we stayed in contact. When he was stuck on a case that involved corporate espionage, he called me. I asked if I could take a crack at it and offer him information. He took me up on it and I gave him all the messages that I received. It turned out that everything I told him was correct and the information that the spirit world offered me helped to lead them in a different direction, which led to an arrest. It didn't take long for word to spread that I was the new medium in town, which also meant that I was being inundated with police cases—with many requests coming directly from the victims' families, not from law enforcement. I, however, decided that I would only work with law enforcement or with police approval. That was until I began to receive phone calls from random police departments all over the United States asking for my assistance with psychic detective work. I never really knew how it started, but I knew who, and although I don't believe in coincidences, the randomness of the contact was welcome and fed into my passion for helping others. I thought perhaps I'd been put into that situation when I was seven so that I could help law enforcement, and possibly even prevent a tragedy. There were several that came and went. Some police agencies helped me with feedback and validations, others simply took down my psychic profile of the situation and thanked me for my time, never calling to mention the outcome. Each case pulled at my heart strings, and still does. I even had to turn down some cases just because I was already pulled in so many directions, and I wasn't receiving a paycheck from any of the departments. Honestly, how do you explain to the taxpayers that there is a psychic on the payroll? I almost became obsessed with the cases to the point that it was interfering with my real job. And the case of Jessi was no different.

The cell phone chimed as I sat at my desk. The glares from my coworkers were obvious. Cell phones were a no-no in my office. I quickly glanced down at the screen and answered it.

"Kristy, I need your help," Paul begged.

Paul was a no-nonsense detective. He was a devoted Catholic, a father of several children, and a guy who hated to have cold cases. I had worked with him on a couple cases for the past couple months, but there was one that had gone cold and it was haunting him.

"Hold on a second," I answered back. "I'm going to take a break right now," I told the receptionist. "I'll be right back."

I snuck into the break room, plopped on the couch, and unmuted the caller.

"Paul, what's up?" I asked. I felt like one of Charlie's Angels every time I heard his voice, my heart beating quickly.

"We arrested someone and I need you to take a look at his photo to tell me what you get. You call that a vibe, right?"

"Uh, sort of. I would call it a feeling or an intuitive hit," I answered, feeling a bit uneasy. I never had an easy time explaining exactly how I received the messages. "I'm at work right now, but you can send it to my email. Can I call you when I get off of work?"

"That will be fine. You know you can call me anytime."

The phone clicked dead. Paul never said goodbye.

I was excited as I went back to my desk. This wasn't my first rodeo. But that happy feeling soon left as soon as I sat down in my gray computer chair.

"The boss wants to see you in his office."

My boss had been a principal and talking to him always made me feel as if I was a kid. It was never good to be called into his office. I closed my eyes, said a quick prayer, and knocked on his door.

"Come in. And close the door behind you."

I did as instructed and stood in front of his desk. Never good with eye contact, he continued plucking at the keyboard as he lectured.

"Your cell phone rang again."

"Yes, I'm sorry." I started to explain, but was immediately cut off.

"You know the rules."

"Yes, sir," I said, bowing my head.

"Sit down, Kristy."

I did so on command, knowing that I was in trouble.

"I did a search of your computer, and I don't know what you're involved in, Kristy, but I want it to stop. Now."

I was stunned. I felt exposed. I felt violated. I never improperly used the work computer. I was a rules girl, after all.

I only used my computer during breaks or at lunchtime, so I was sick that he ran a scan of my computer. So did he know? Or was he making assumptions? What exactly did he know?

"You can go now, Kristy."

Tears sprung to my eyes as I sat down at my desk to finish my day. The adrenaline that I felt from the call from Paul was all but forgotten, and I felt exposed and raw. I had a workers' compensation report to prepare for the board of education.

Five o'clock finally came, and I wasn't even in my car before the cell phone rang. The persistent detective again.

"What do you think?" he asked.

"The boss chewed me out and I wasn't able to look. I'm sorry, Paul. I'm on my way home and will take a look-see. Call you tomorrow?"

"No, call me anytime tonight. Even if it's midnight. You can always call me, Kristy."

Click.

The crappy day faded, and I was on a mission once more.

After feeding the family and pets, watering the plants, and changing into some comfortable sweats, I sat down at the laptop and opened my email box. Junk, more junk, spam mail, an overdue bill, and finally Paul's email. Again, there were no frills—only a picture and the police record of a potential killer.

As I reviewed the information, I realized that this was what I loved doing. It wasn't data entry, or state reports, or payroll. The meeting in my boss's office had made me real-ize that, although the job served its purpose at the time, it was also time to serve a purpose. I had to make a change, but how and when I wasn't sure.

"Can you meet with me this weekend, Kristy? We need to find this girl."

"I don't know." I hesitated. "My mom's pretty sick, Paul."

"For just one day. Please."

I knew that if Paul was asking politely, he truly needed my assistance. He had been with the department for over twenty years and, although on the outside he looked just as tough as he sounded, his soul was soft and loving.

"Yep, see you Saturday."

———

A photograph of a pretty twenty-something girl with long brown hair and brown eyes sat in front of me on the gray conference table. Although the photograph was taken in happier times, noted by her smile and her sparkling eyes, it lacked life. She had gotten herself into some trouble, into a bad crowd, and it had become her demise. I tried to see if my spirit guides could find her on the Other Side, but they shook their heads. She hadn't crossed over. Her physical body still needed to be found in order for her to have closure. I put my head in my hands and shook my head, tears streaming down my face. I was afraid to look at anybody. Being the bearer of bad news was just one of the crappy parts of my job, a job that I wasn't even getting paid to do. But Jessi's family was just outside Paul's office door, and I was going to have to face them.

"So you think she's dead?" Paul asked, looking down at his cell phone. His office was in the basement of an old building, in an old town. His office light flickered. "Just a train going by," he explained without emotion.

"She's definitely not living, Paul."

"Kristy, can you start from the beginning? This time, I'll tape it."

I nodded as Paul grabbed his tape recorder, popping in a tape and hitting record. "Just take it slowly," he said softly.

"It was Tuesday night and I had just gotten the kids to bed and laid down myself. I have been having problems at work and was overly stressed out, so I thought that I would flip channels..."

"Kristy, do you do drugs, take medication, or drink?" the detective interrupted, scribbling on his yellow legal pad.

I grinned. This was the typical cop question, and I didn't blame them. I was cleaner than a whistle and politely answered his questions. I didn't like to drink and it was rare for me to even take a sip of wine. Drugs? I had never even smoked a *cigarette* and taking drugs was unthinkable. I joked that I didn't need spirits to see spirits, and I couldn't imagine what would happen if I took drugs.

"I just had to check," the detective solemnly replied. "Keep going."

I nodded and continued. "After turning on the television, it was mere minutes before I fell asleep, but was quickly awakened by someone shaking my right shoulder. I assumed that it was one of the kids, so I peeked. Instead of my kids, there was a girl in her early twenties standing over my bedside, looking frightened."

"How did you know that it was a ghost and not really her?"

"To me, spirits look different than the living. They look…grayer. And depending upon the way they died, they take on a different shade of gray or white," I tried to explain, but felt as if I was rambling.

Paul nodded, although I could tell he was still confused. I took a cleansing breath, in through my nose and out from my mouth, and continued. "Even though I've seen spirits since I was a little girl, I still get startled. I pushed myself up in the bed and grabbed my notebook and pen that I always keep on the nightstand. I went through my usual questioning, asking her name, who she was, what she wanted, how I could help her, etc. She told me that her name was Jessi and…" I began to choke up. I looked at Paul, who could tell that I was having a hard time. Death, no matter whose it is, isn't an easy topic, and feeling like the messenger of death…well, sometimes it was too much to handle.

"Kristy, why don't you instead write out a statement?"

"Absolutely," I answered, relieved. "I would also like to draw you a map to the location where I believe she is, but I must forewarn you—I'm not a great artist and it will be quite rough."

After forty-five minutes, I had completed my assignments and was placed in the passenger seat of the undercover police car on my way to a location that resembled my chicken scratch. I had seen gory ghosts, individuals who had died in a way that no human being should. They've stood over my bed looking like something out of a horror film. Arm missing, blood everywhere, eye gouged. I had also seen horrible pictures from the coroner and dead bodies, but it still didn't get any easier, and I wasn't sure how I was going to handle standing graveside as an innocent person was dug up from the earth.

As we rounded the entrance to the park, Paul's cell phone rang. I didn't even have to hear the words he spoke; his eyes told it all. Jessi's body was found lying in a field next to an old metal garage. He snapped his phone shut, quietly nodded, and turned the car around, driving me back to his office.

"Now," Paul said, "we find the killer."

All I could do was nod and pray that Jessi could finally cross over to the Other Side and find some sort of peace.

Monday morning I came back to work, happy that I helped put Jessi to rest, but sad that there are so many monsters that have no consideration for human life. My coworkers could never figure out why I got so exhausted on weekends. Working police cases became an exhilarating part of my life. My vacation time from work was spent looking for dead bodies and touring the United States trying to be the crime solver, only I am well aware of who the heroes actually are—the detectives. Nope, psychics or mediums don't solve cases, the police do. In my stack of papers on my desk was a probation notice from my boss that I needed to sign. I was going to have to figure out soon what I wanted to do, and figure it out fast.

Jessi still visits me from time to time, deep in the night, and I continue to stay in contact with her family, as I do with most all of my clients from police cases.

There are some jobs that you can leave at the office. This is one job that follows me through my nightmares.

# twenty-one

# Voices

Dating someone with kids and having to explain what I did was interesting. Thankfully, the kids were intrigued, not appalled. Chuck and I often spent our Friday evenings ghost hunting and researching haunted locations. When he and his girls invited Connor, Micaela, and me to Minnesota for a week on their family's farm to visit, we were excited. We all needed a break and thought it would be interesting to see how our families handled a twelve-hour trip to Minnesota. And I'd get a chance to meet Uncle Bob and Aunt Kathy. The girls were most excited to show me the haunted home that the family owned.

———————

"But I *heard* them with my own ears!! There were children upstairs in the bedroom. I *heard* them calling to me,

Bob! They must have jumped out the window because I couldn't find them when I went to look for them. Are they here?" The agitated elderly lady looked up at her middle-aged son, anxiously wringing her hands in worry.

"No, Mom, they're not here," Bob said, rubbing the sleep out of his eyes. "There *are* no children. Let me drive you back home so that we can all get some sleep. It's late. We'll discuss this more in the morning over coffee."

Slipping his brown loafers on his feet and tying his robe tighter around his robust belly, he gently took his mother's elbow and guided her out the door toward the car.

The almost full moon hovered in the velvet canvas of stars, cascading light upon the Minnesota farmland. To the south, soft waves crashed upon the shore of Lobster Lake.

"I'm telling you that I heard them. I was *not* dreaming. I was wide awake. They were giggling and whispering. Oh my, what if they're by the lake or lost in the cornfields? Bob, we have to go look for them!"

Bob's mom's eyes glowed crazy with worry. She darted away from the open car door.

Bob lightly caught her shoulder. "I'll look for them after I take you home, Mom," he said with a yawn. "Promise me that you will call me instead of wandering out in the night. Kathy and I worry about you."

During the short drive to the old farmhouse, Bob's mom looked out the passenger side window into the darkness, searching for signs of the missing children.

"Promise me, Mom."

She continued to peer out into the blackness as he led her into the house.

"I mean it!" Bob said.

"I promise," she wearily agreed.

"Everything okay, hon?" Kathy asked, snuggling up to Bob as he crawled back into bed.

"Mom again," he sighed heavily.

"Is she still hearing voices?"

"Yes. It seems to be getting worse. We *have* to find a place for her. I just cannot take any more chances. She could fall into the lake or hurt herself running over here or ...who knows what else!"

"We'll call around in the morning," Kathy mumbled sleepily.

---

"There it is," Chuck pointed out the front of windshield. "There's Aunt Kathy and Uncle Bob's house!"

"And there is the haunted farmhouse! Dagney's old house." Cora spoke up, pointing to the white farmhouse that stood east of the more contemporary home that Chuck had pointed to.

"Haunted?" I smirked. "It looks like a cute house. Not spooky at all."

"Just wait," Chuck warned with a grin.

The crackle of the stones under the car tires signaled our arrival and the homeowners met us in the driveway.

"Aunt Kathy. Uncle Bob. Meet my new girlfriend Kristy and her kids Micaela and Connor."

I offered a hug to each and proceeded to stretch. After the long trip from Michigan to Minnesota, everybody in the car was stiff. Chuck's kids, Cora and Molly, scooted out of the car and "how big you have grown" remarks were shared, along with more hugs and kisses.

"Can we take Micaela and Connor down to the lake?" Cora asked her dad.

"Yes, but be careful," Chuck warned the kids as they ran off down to the water, barely waiting for his approval.

After carrying the luggage into the house and to our respective rooms, the adults sat down at the dining room table, overlooking the rolling farmland out the door.

"So, Kristy, Chuck tells me that you're a psychic," Aunt Kathy said, looking inquisitive.

"I prefer intuitive, but yes...I am a psychic. Not professionally, mind you. I have a *real* job, too." I laughed nervously, pouring a soft drink into a glass and taking a sip.

"Well, I can't wait to take you over to Uncle Bob's mom's house to see what you think. The kids think it is haunted." Aunt Kathy laughed.

I laughed with her. It seemed that once people found out I was a psychic, everybody had some haunted story and I remained a skeptic. Intrigued, but still skeptical.

Chuck and the kids had told me stories of the abandoned farmhouse, or Dagney's house as they called it. There had been no scientific evidence of a haunting, merely just a feeling that they got when they were in there. In fact, the house was completely furnished, yet nobody would stay in it because of that eerie feeling.

After a few days into the vacation, the gang decided to visit the "haunted" home. The sun was still high in the Minnesota sky as Chuck, Aunt Kathy, and all the kids led the way through the fields over to the house. Unlocking the door, Aunt Kathy stepped back and let Chuck and me enter before her.

"So...do you feel anything?" Chuck and Aunt Kathy both asked in unison as they all entered the kitchen.

I laughed. "Give me some time to actually *see* the house."

Straight through the kitchen was the dining room, furnished with a beautiful antique dining set. To the right of the dining room was a living room boasting a couch, chairs, and a piano. But the most startling, most eerie part of the living room was hanging on the wall—a painting of a young woman with black hair, large eyes, and a sober expression. Perpendicular to the painting was a small mirror reflecting the painting, yet the face in mirror took on an entirely new look—gray hair and hollow eyes. I jumped back at the sight.

"See?" Cora grinned. "Spooky, huh?"

"There has to be an explanation. The lighting or something," I said and continued on, moving slowly through the other rooms.

Accessible through both the master bedroom and the living room was a bathroom. I stopped, feeling an odd, closed-throat feeling.

"The cellar is through this trap door here," Aunt Kathy said, pointing to the access panel in the bathroom. "Do you want to go down there?"

"Sure, but only if someone will accompany me."

"I've got your back," Chuck said as he pulled the door open and turned on switch that would light the way.

Carefully and slowly, we climbed down the steep stairway. Jars of canned food lined the long stone wall. And although a dirt floor was the foundation, the basement was remarkably clean of cobwebs and dust. Cora snapped pictures from the bathroom above. A thick sense of evil was felt, and my chest began to feel tight, as if someone were sitting on it.

"Let's get out of here," Chuck said while looking around, his face turning white. "This wall should not be boarded up like this," Chuck added, pointing at the wall behind the furnace. "Something doesn't feel right."

Chuck put his hand on my shoulders and steered me to the steps and we once again carefully and slowly climbed up until we reached the bathroom.

"Well?" the group asked in unison.

"It definitely has a strange feel to it down there," I replied, trying to sound skeptical so as not to scare the kids.

"Why don't we go upstairs?" Aunt Kathy said, walking toward the stairwell.

"Mom, I'm having hard time breathing," Micaela whispered, her blue eyes shining with fear.

"Why don't you and Connor go outside? I won't be long."

"I'd rather stay with you. I'll be okay, I just feel strange," Micaela stated and began climbing the steps with the rest of the group.

Molly whispered to Aunt Kathy, "Micaela and Connor are both sensitive, too."

The upstairs had two bedrooms and a bathroom. Nothing unusual was felt in the bathroom, but upon entering the first bedroom, I began to choke back tears. Images of a young girl being raped in the closet ran painfully through my head. Emotions from the young girl's ordeal were strongly felt and I ushered Micaela and Connor quickly to the next room, without a word to anybody. The next room had a sense of oddness to it also, but held no apparent explanation why.

An old orchard grew between the houses. Old, beautiful trees cascaded down, creating shadows upon the family as they walked back home.

Connor raced up to me. "Mom? Why do I feel like someone is following me and yet nobody is behind me?"

"I don't know, hon," I replied with a hug, "but nothing can hurt you. Mom won't let that happen."

Connor, satisfied with the answer, raced to catch up with the girls, who were already near the porch.

"Aunt Kathy, would it be okay if Chuck and I came back to the farmhouse later tonight? Without the kids."

Aunt Kathy nodded and said that she would leave the key with Chuck in case they were not home. "Is there is something wrong?" she asked.

"Wrong? Well, I can give you my impressions, but can you wait until I sit down and try and gather all of my thoughts?"

"Of course."

I went to take a hot shower, water being a sanctuary for thought, and tried to come up with a politically correct way to state my impressions.

With the kids down by the water playing and out of earshot, Chuck, Aunt Kathy, Uncle Bob, and I once again sat around the dining room table.

"Well," I began, "I was skeptical. Do I think the house is haunted? I don't know, but I definitely can you give you some of my impressions. First, that picture in the living room gives me the creeps and there's something in the basement that was bothering me. Is there a room that's blocked off down there?"

Uncle Bob nodded. "Yes, I do believe there is. They did that when they put the new furnace in. I'm not sure why, though."

I thought for a moment on how to voice the next statement. "My main impression, though"—I hesitated again—"is in the closet in the first bedroom upstairs. I sensed that a young girl was taken advantage of against her will."

Uncle Bob and Aunt Kathy both nodded.

"Yes, that did happen. I didn't know *where* in the house, but…I will trust that you know more than I do. We don't speak of that incident, as you might understand."

"The other strange feeling that I got was when we passed the orchard. I know that Connor also was picking up on something. Do you happen to know why I felt a presence there?"

"Well," Uncle Bob began, "the original farmhouse stood in front of that orchard. I believe that there was a fire in the late 1800s that burned it to the ground and the house you were just at was built in its place."

"Interesting. I'll see if I pick up anything tonight without having to worry about the kids."

"Kristy! Dad! Look at this!" Cora came running in from the backyard. "I was looking at the pictures that I took at the farmhouse. Look."

She handed the camera to me and I hit Review. Scrolling through the many pictures, I saw several photos that displayed orbs, yet they were only apparent in the shots that the kids were in. In the basement, a picture of a face, against the wall, was as clear as day.

"Freaky," I responded. Once again trying not get hyped up.

"Can Molly and I *please* go with you later?"

Chuck and I looked at one another. Micaela was ten years old and Connor eight. But Cora and Molly were older, being sixteen and thirteen, respectively.

Sighing deeply, Chuck agreed to let the girls go, but not until Connor and Micaela were settled in for the night with a movie to watch, preferably a non-scary movie.

Once night fell, the group of four set out on the expedition. Carrying a flashlight and two cameras, Molly, Cora,

Chuck, and I walked across the field toward the white farm-house, the full moon brightly lighting the way. Passing in front of the orchard, I once again felt a sense of panic in my chest, but continued on trying to look inconspicuous. And just as Connor had described, I too felt like someone was watching me from the grove.

Unlocking the door, we entered and turned on the kit-chen light. Walking through the dining room to the living room, I thought that once again the portrait of the woman seemed to have changed her expression from earlier in the day, yet the image in the mirror remained the same as what was on the wall. As Chuck walked through the rest of the house to turn on the overhead lights, his flashlight stopped working. No matter how much he banged it, it would not come back to life. He shrugged, since the lights were now on. The energy in the house was thick as the group toured the farmhouse again. Too frightened of the cellar and without a light source, I bowed out of venturing downstairs, and instead made my way upstairs with everyone else following close behind. Once again, the strong emotion of past activities in the closet hit hard and I began to tear up. It was then that Chuck noticed the blankets on the bed moving, as if someone was sitting on the bed. Molly straightened the bedclothes out, but after a few seconds they again made impressions. Startled and unsure as to what was making the movement, everyone went into the other bedroom, where the same phenomenon was witnessed.

"Someone is definitely trying to make us aware of their presence!" I stated.

"I cannot get my camera to work," Cora complained.

I tried mine. "Me neither. It's got brand-new batteries, too."

"Same here." Cora nodded.

Molly and Cora's eyes grew wide as they looked around for more signs, but the energy seemed to settle down, so the group decided to go back down to the first floor and call it a night. Holding tightly to the railing, I led the way down the steep stairway. Feeling someone bump up against me, I turned around to urge cautiousness; however, the closest person was still three stairs up above me.

"Did you hear that?" Chuck questioned.

"Hear what? All I know is that I felt someone bump into me. But nobody bumped into me," I said, stopping in my tracks in the middle of the steps.

"I hear children downstairs," Chuck answered, "back by the laundry room."

Soft giggles from the first floor carried up the stairwell.

"Maybe Micaela and Connor came over to scare us," Cora offered.

"Maybe," both Chuck and I replied in unison, not sounding a bit convinced.

Chuck made his way toward the laundry room with me following behind.

"I'm having a hard time breathing all of a sudden," I said and quickly walked back to the living room with the kids, trying to catch my breath.

"I'll go with Dad," Molly said, and courageously ran ahead, but just as I had, quickly returning complaining of not being able to catch her breath.

"I cannot see them," Chuck called out from the other room, "but I can still hear them. It is as if they are taunt..."

Before Chuck finished his sentence, the phone rang; one loud shrill. Our group ran to the kitchen door, holding tight to one another in fear. After a second, all erupted into fits of giggles from the silliness of being scared of the telephone.

"Good one, Uncle Bob. Fabulous timing!" Chuck chuckled. "I *did* hear kids' voices, though."

Everybody nodded. Everybody else had heard them too.

Still high on the adrenaline of the scare, we walked toward the living room once more, only to again be stopped in our tracks again.

"Over here," a child giggled, and then one single high note on the piano played as all looked on.

"What the..." Cora began.

"And I think that is our note to leave," I joked. "We have spooked ourselves enough to last us awhile. I think there is a lot of activity here. More than what we can deal with ourselves and I don't want anybody getting hurt. I think we should just leave," I said seriously.

Just as we went to walk out the door, the rotary phone shrilled again and the group screeched. Instead of answering, everybody silently slid out the back door, locked the door, and began the journey back home.

"Odd," Chuck said, breaking the silence. "Flashlight works now."

"So does my camera," I added, flipping the switch.

"Mine too," Cora said, doing the same.

"So? What did you find?" Connor and Micaela asked, greeting us at the door.

"Isn't it way past your bedtime?" I scolded. "Go back to bed and I'll be there in a few minutes to tuck you in."

Hesitantly, the kids closed the hall door and headed solemnly to their bedrooms.

"The kids have been very concerned about you, so we let them stay up," Aunt Kathy said. "So, did you find anything?"

"Well, you both pulled some great pranks on us," Chuck said, laughing.

Aunt Kathy and Uncle Bob looked innocently at the family. "What do you mean?" Uncle Bob asked.

The activities of the night were explained in depth, with all adding their own flavor to it.

"We promise that we did not go over to the house. Micaela and Connor can vouch for us on that one," Uncle Bob said.

"We promise. We've been here the whole time!" Connor chimed in, eavesdropping from the hallway with Micaela in tow.

"Well, you called us, right?" Chuck laughed, still trying to shake off the adrenaline.

"The phone? The phone has been disconnected for over three years, Chuck!" Bob said, shaking his head.

"Wait, are you telling me that you actually heard voices of children?" Aunt Kathy asked, looking pale.

"Yes, we all did," Chuck stated.

"So," Aunt Kathy said, turning to Uncle Bob, "maybe Mom wasn't going crazy after all. Maybe we shouldn't have doubted her. Maybe Mom really did hear children's voices."

"Now what do we do?" Bob asked, also looking pale.

"We go to bed," I said, "and look at everything again in the morning. The spirits seem to be content in the house. We can let them be or I can try and get them to cross over. But for now...we sleep."

Two small dark shadows looked out in the night over the family's land, giggled mischievously, and vanished.

The haunting of the home in Minnesota was never solved, as Chuck's aunt and uncle decided to just tear it down and lay the spirits to rest. Our whole family still talks of the experience with an unsettled feeling. Although the home is gone, that doesn't necessarily mean that the spirits have crossed over.

# twenty-two

# Amber Rose

My nights are filled with spirits and ghosts lining up to speak with me. Some nights I am successful in turning them down, but most nights I am the counselor to the dead. It was just a few months after Jessi's case when another spirit visited me. Unlike the others, her energy had a sense of urgency.

"You can see me?"

The pretty girl stood next to my bed. I could hear Chuck snoring on the couch and voices from the television set. The baseball game that he had been watching probably ended several hours ago. I could just visualize him falling asleep sitting up, remote still grasped tightly in his hand. I rubbed my eyes to make certain that I wasn't dreaming, yet even after I sat up in bed, the spirit still stood there. She had dirty blonde hair and some piercings and was wearing a pink T-shirt and worn-out jeans.

"How long have you been gone?" I asked, grabbing the notepad and pen that sat on my nightstand.

She sighed and shook her head. "I'm not even sure. I don't think it's been long."

I looked hard at her to see her aura. It was white with a dull gray shadow, which showed me that she had made it through the light to the Other Side, but still had unresolved issues. And boy did she have unresolved issues.

"Can you tell me what happened to you ... uh, what is your name?"

"Amber Rose," she said, beginning to cry. "Really just Amber, but my mom would call me Amber Rose—I even got a tattoo of a rose on my hip." She pulled her pants slightly down so that I could see the image on her hip.

"What happened?"

"My boyfriend murdered me and buried my body."

She looked all of sixteen years old with a hardness that only the streets could give.

"I don't mean to be insensitive, Amber, but in order to help you, I need more information than that."

In what was probably only a half hour, she described the location and kept saying over and over that it was where she and her boyfriend would go all the time. It was not in Michigan, but she had family in Michigan.

After mulling over what I was going to do with the information, I decided to try something I never did. I got up in the morning and typed into the search engine on the computer, "Amber. Missing." This instantly produced her name and a website noting that she was in fact missing and her family only lived a hop and a skip from me.

I gasped, looking at her picture on the screen, at the uncanny resemblance, only my visitor had more brown in her hair. (Maybe there isn't hair dye on the Other Side?) I plugged in the information for Crime Stoppers and sent off an email similar to, "I swear I am perfectly sane, but I am a spirit medium and would like to assist the family with Amber's case. Free of charge." And just hours after sending the email, Amber's mother called to inform me that her cousin was now handling the case because she was extremely ill. I would love to say that the weekend resulted in a solved crime, but it took well over a year.

Amber had told me was that she was in (or near) a metro park that had a cemetery in it, and that she was near water, but not in the water.

I immediately bonded with Amber's cousin, Paula. She had a heart of gold and was the glue that held her family together, even though she had an array of health concerns.

Amber's family tried to get the detectives to listen to the information I was receiving, but they would have nothing of it, so her family decided to take matters into their own hands and asked me to come and search the location. Our team consisted of Amber's cousin, sister, father, another psychic medium, Chuck, and me. With several parks in the area, we choose the one that was most desolate.

It wasn't as if we were carrying shovels as we hiked the park—instead I tried to call on Amber to get more information as to where she was buried—but as we hiked further into the park, we were stopped by park officials and questioned. We admitted that we weren't just on a nature walk—we were looking for a dead body. Everybody pointed at me to explain why.

Skeptical, but curious, the deputy director and a park ranger asked me to sit on a picnic bench and write out everything I knew and draw a map. After about fifteen minutes, I handed over the information that Amber had given me.

"Are you sure that you've never been here before?"

"This is my first time," I answered, getting nervous.

"All right, let's take a walk. But only you. Nobody else."

I agreed, although now I wonder what I was thinking. The ranger was none too thrilled with the idea of a medium and he made it known throughout most of the walk.

The director received a phone call and had to walk up a hill to get better reception, leaving me alone with the ranger with attitude. A group of three small boys walked toward us, one cupping his hand.

"What do you have there?" the ranger asked the oldest boy, who looked to be about eight.

"A frog," he replied and proudly unfolded his hand to reveal his treasure.

"Be careful with that."

"I will, sir," the boy replied, carefully holding the frog.

The boys walked passed us and the ranger and I held a gaze. Electricity burned and we both realized that we were deep within the woods where there were three young boys, yet no adults. Both of us swung around to look, only to see the boys dissipate into thin air.

"Was that a ... ?"

I couldn't help but grin. "Must've been."

"I believe you," he said, shaking his head. "Yup, I believe you."

If only I could convince every skeptic in that way.

We later discovered that those three boys had drowned in the nearby river years ago, as they searched for frogs.

The search plodded on and was now well over the two-hour mark. As we walked, they asked me questions about the case, along with others in their area. I abruptly stopped.

"What do you see?"

"The trees," I pointed. "The trees where Amber is aren't this dark in color. They are a lighter pine."

They looked at one another knowingly. "Anything else?"

"I know this is going to sound weird, but does this park have a cemetery?"

"No, but there is one that does, and it just so happens to be behind the home of the boyfriend's father."

It didn't take a psychic to put the rest of the puzzle together after that. We stood there downloading the information that I shared, trying to figure out our next move.

The other message Amber gave me was concrete, but nobody could make head or tail on what that clue meant.

We decided to set a later date to search the other park with K-9s in tow.

It would be several months before we could make another visit, and this time it was only Chuck, Paula, and me. We once again made the three-hour trek back to search.

Pulling up to the park, I had shivers. I knew we were where she was. Asking for her guidance, we began. As we rounded the curve to where the small cemetery sat, I began to cry. I nodded to continue on. It was well over ninety degrees and I had worn shorts and a tank top, which was really not hiking wear. By the end of the search, I was covered in burrs and squealing from the jumping spiders and the snakes that seemed to chase us. We finally got to a destination that felt right, and I stuck a stick in the ground.

"She's right around here. Closer to that way, by the light pine trees and the marshy area." I pointed. I had felt water around her, but I never felt that she was in the water. "But that is private property, right?"

The rangers nodded. "By the way, that's the boyfriend's father's home." The lead ranger pointed.

The K-9s were let loose and they indeed responded by sitting near the spot I marked.

"Can we get a warrant, or dig?"

"We wait."

"Wait? Wait for what?"

I was met with a shrug, and we loaded the car up to leave. The search party exchanged hugs and well wishes, but I was left feeling depleted. All that, and we just had to leave?!

Chuck and I made our way to the car when I was suddenly accosted by the media.

"Psychic says she knows where Amber is," the lead story on the five o'clock local news aired, playing a clip of me wishing the family closure and rushing away.

The last thing I wanted was media attention. Amber's killer was on the loose, and I was still getting used to my newfound title of medium.

That night we stayed in a shady-looking hotel. I was awake the entire night hearing Amber's cries and feeling as if I were being watched, not by the spirit world, but by evil itself. Headlights shone in our room and I jumped.

"We have to go home, Chuck," I begged. "I think he knows we're here! We should leave now!" But it was well after midnight, and after eight hours of hiking through miles of woodland, the last thing Chuck wanted to do was pack up and hit the road in the middle of the night.

He assured me that we were safe and reminded me that I had a meeting with a private investigator in the morning regarding another missing persons case in Columbus.

I slept fully dressed, holding my cell phone close in case I needed to dial 911, and clung to Chuck.

Leaving the area was once again heartbreaking. I wasn't concerned with breaking open the case or catching the killer; my goal was finding Amber and putting her to rest. But, once again, we were leaving without doing that.

Three months later, four years after Amber's death, Amber's mom passed away. Between her various illnesses and her broken heart, her body just couldn't hold up. Amber's father lost himself in grief and her sister felt orphaned. A couple days after Christmas day in 2007, not long after Amber's mom's passing, I received the call that Amber's boyfriend, Rickie, went on a killing spree that included strangling his mother and beating her boyfriend to death with a shovel. Rickie was missing, and anybody associated with the case had to be on the lookout as there had been more mysterious missing people, suicides, and murders associated with the case. We were all on edge. I was petrified to leave my house until I heard word that he was caught. Just a few days later, I received the call that they found him, at the very same hotel that we had stayed at just a few months ago. And a few days afterwards, the deputy director called to tell me that they found Amber's remains, just steps away from where I had placed the stick marking her grave. Three years after I took on the case, Amber's murderer had his day in court, where prosecutors released the information that after she was killed, she was transferred several times and finally buried with concrete poured atop to prevent any cadaver dogs from finding her.

Amber is now at peace with her mother, and justice has been served. I, however, am saddened at how many people had to lose their lives at the hands of a handsome monster. If detectives had pressured her boyfriend some more, maybe his mom and her boyfriend would still be alive, along with the string of others who perished mysteriously.

# twenty-three

# Confessions

As I was running around playing Nancy Drew, my mom was dying and I couldn't do anything about it. She had survived the first year after the heart attack, but on January 3, the day I returned back to work after Christmas vacation, she had another heart attack and was in bad shape. The decision loomed for our family. Do we sign off on her having heart surgery and more than likely dying, or not have the surgery and almost certainly dying? We decided to do whatever we could and pray for a miracle.

That Christmas I had splurged and bought her a cashmere sweater. For years on end she talked about wanting a cashmere sweater. I sobbed thinking about the memories that still hadn't been made—memories that mattered. I didn't want to lose her.

It was a brisk January morning when I was called at work and drove to the hospital to sit next to my mom's bedside. I knew that I had to come clean with her.

"Mom, I know how much you hated when I was a little girl that I saw spirits and ghosts, but I'm doing that as a career now. I work with the police and I'm doing readings."

We spent over an hour talking about it. She made me feel accepted for the first time in my life. She asked me to give her details of the cases, and gratefully I did. Her blind eyes shone bright with the fear of the next day's surgery.

"Kristy, if you're psychic, you also know if I am going to make it, right?"

"Mom, you're going to be just fine," I said, kissing her gently on her cheek, choking back the lie.

The rest of the morning, we tried to keep things light and rambled about the kids and their activities, weather reports, and I kept her laughing with anecdotes about my cat Ozzy and dog Guinness. I spared her any conversations on my mounting bills or the boss who was giving me problems for taking so much time off. I merely held her hand in mine and talked like there wasn't a worry in the world. Every so often a nurse would come in to explain details of the next day's open-heart surgery or to check on her vitals. We laughed and talked about everything and anything. She cried her heart out when I went home, and I cried all the way to the car because I knew that this would be our last real time together.

Mom and I were close, but we had a love/hate relationship. Her stubbornness and moodiness drove me crazy. My stubbornness and moodiness drove her crazy. We agreed to disagree in order to get along, but even through the worst arguments, we always made up.

I kept a busy life, so even though we lived but miles away from one another, I wasn't always able to go over to her house every week. However, no matter what, I called her on my way home from work every day. Most of the time I kept my worries private, as my mom fed off of them and worried enough for the both of us. She was an empath in her own right, but when I needed a hug, she was there to give me one.

The morning of the surgery, I was a nervous wreck and I knew that my mom was just as nervous. Walking down the hallway, I heard a familiar voice in my mom's room. "The police? She's lying." I heard my brother laugh. "She always did have an imagination." I never heard my mom's response. I walked into the room, my cheeks flaming with what I suppose could only be labeled humiliation. The dreaded curse again. The acceptance I felt from the day before was quickly replaced with loneliness.

In the early morning of January 30, 2006, I received a phone call urging me to get over to the hospital. I had just pulled into work, but instead of waiting for the elevator, I ran up the three flights of stairs to let my boss know that I was there, but had to leave. I didn't give any explanation; I just raced back down the stairs, to the car. I couldn't cry, something not typical for me. On my way to the hospital I called Chuck, who said he'd meet me there. As I drove the twenty or so miles, I sensed my mom sitting in the passenger seat next to me and I asked for a sign.

The ride to the hospital was numbing. Every song on the radio was cheerful and happy. I didn't want to hear cheerful and happy. I was determined to hurt, so I switched it over to the country station, and there was my sign. Brooks and Dunn were singing a song called "I Believe." I knew that mom had crossed, and she was telling me she was fine.

As I rode the elevator up to mom's room, I could feel her next to me telling me not to cry. She never liked to see me crying. Dad was by mom's side, holding her hand. My brother stood over her body, sobbing. I came up to her and gave her a kiss when my dad told me that she had passed. I already *knew*. I just nodded and told her that I loved her and sat down on the floor. Dad looked at me and told me to choose a funeral home. I knew then that I had to be the one to hold it all together and take control.

At the age of sixty-eight, Sally Lou Schiller gave up her fight. Now, even though she cannot show me how to make her famous chicken noodle soup, I know for sure that she looks at us from above and knows what her grandchildren look like, knows what I look like, and can finally read my books.

Planning the funeral was a welcome distraction, yet each afternoon, I reached for the phone to call my mom and then remembered.

One of the things she used to tell us was that she hated gladiolas and referred to them as a funeral flower. "Don't let those yucky flowers be at my funeral," she would say. So my sister and I carefully chose every single flower for her arrangement. She loved wildflowers, so we themed her arrangements in pinks, blues, and purples. Dad asked me to choose her outfit. Knowing how much she loved to be comfortable—"Kristy, just dress me in my nightgown in my casket," she would tell me—I chose a comfortable pink sweater and a black velvet skirt, plus fuzzy pink socks. She looked beautiful and comfortable. I didn't have the heart to bury her in the cashmere sweater that still had tags attached and was sitting in her bedroom dresser.

The day before the funeral was her visitation. It was a long day of meeting friends and family. She used to say that nobody would ever attend her funeral, but it was packed full. I only wish she had the same reception when she was alive. Her depression and her blindness had made her into a social hermit, and many people, relatives and friends alike, had abandoned her. At least that is how she felt. At the end of the evening, my entire office came to show their support. It choked me up with gratitude.

My boss offered his sympathy, and my son, who was nine years old, looked up at him and brazenly asked if he was going to fire me.

"Why would you say that?" my boss said, appalled.

Work gave me an awful time for taking time off to be with my mom—I had been written up, and I was even told that they called the hospital to make sure I was telling the truth. I didn't believe that I had even said anything out loud, but Connor had obviously picked up on the stress.

"Now do you believe her?" Connor asked my boss, pointing to his dead grandmother.

My boss turned red and bent down to Connor to reassure him that my job was safe.

Regardless if my job was safe or not, I wasn't happy. Years back I'd thought it was my dream job, but all of the years of resentment had taken its toll.

The funeral was early the next morning. I looked through the flowers and cards and then stopped in my tracks. One of the arrangements was a bouquet of gladiolas. I pointed it out to my dad, who told me that we couldn't remove it as the person who gave it was going to be there, and so at the feet of my mom's casket sat the dreaded funeral flowers.

The service began and I could see the spirit of my mom standing next to the shell of her body. She looked brilliantly happy and she waved to me. I blew her a kiss and broke down in tears. Then smack dab in the middle of the message, the arrangement of gladiola blooms fell over. Laughter erupted from those who knew that mom had to have her way.

Just a week after my mom's passing, I was heading home from the office when I had a strong pull to stop into the cemetery, but not the cemetery where my mom's physical body was. Instead I was drawn to the cemetery where my grandparents were buried. I tend to not go to cemeteries (except for ghost hunting) just because I don't need to—I can speak to them anywhere and know they will hear me. I listened to my intuition, however, and dutifully drove in. With only my memory of where their gravestones were, I found the draping pine tree and parked. Sitting on the ground near their stone, I had an instant flashback of when I was all of eight years old and my grandpa had passed away. I saw the funeral, those in attendance, and felt the sadness of everybody—especially of my mom. Tears began to fall and I wondered why I had been drawn to feeling that sadness. A bird chirped above me, nudging me from my sorrow, and it was then that I saw her. Sitting in a lawn chair with a baby boy was a beautiful woman. She held the boy's hand and stared at the grave. It was obvious that the funeral was recent because cascades of flowers were freshly laid on the dirt mound. I sat for bit, wondering if my sorrow was more hers than of my own past memory. Before I could conjure an answer, the little boy quickly crawled down from the chair and toddled over to me, plopping himself down in my lap. I was startled. He looked up at me and smiled a knowing smile. I tousled his hair, gathered him up, and walked over to mom who was as stunned as I was. She apologized and sat back down with the blond-haired boy in her lap. Her emotions were static in the air. I asked if she was okay and if she wanted to talk.

A young widow with a toddler poured her heart out to me—a perfect stranger. I listened. I cried. I hugged her. I didn't tell her who I was; I wasn't at the cemetery to drum up business. I believe that my grandpa, who was such a bright light, knew that this young girl needed someone to talk to and knew that I was just the person.

As I left the cemetery that evening, I could see my grand-father's spirit standing against the tree by his headstone, smiling. My forever protector.

# twenty-four

# Follow Your Moonstones

The summer after Mom crossed, I took out a map of the United States. I told the family that wherever I pointed was where we were going to vacation that summer. So I closed my eyes, spun myself around, and pointed. I just know that they were praying for Orlando and chanting Disney, Disney, Disney in their minds. Instead, my finger happened to fall upon Solomon's Island, Maryland. The family looked at me like I was crazy, but I asked them to trust me and squinted at my guides and angels, hoping they were leading me correctly.

I researched the area and searched out lodging. I found a cottage on Chesapeake Bay that promised a hot tub, the ocean within walking distance, and Baltimore and Washington, D.C., in close proximity. Nobody was convinced, including Chuck. They had all been praying my finger would land on something a bit more exciting than nowhere land,

Maryland. The kids asked me continually, the weeks before the trip, "Who vacations in Maryland?" I just smiled and prepared. I had a strong feeling this trip was going to be life changing, but I wasn't sure as to how or when. Still, I trusted my instincts.

I had received a recent promotion at my job, and yet I still felt as if I was wandering. The promotion didn't feel right. The place didn't feel right, and, to be honest, I felt lost. Two days before we were supposed to go on the trip, my boss called me into her office and told me that I couldn't go. I just about burst into tears, and after showing her the nonrefundable contract on the cottage, my employer begrudgingly allowed me to take my vacation.

The family piled into the car, not one of them thrilled with the destination. Cora, the oldest, whined about how she was going to hate it, and probably hate us, for making her go. Again, I grinned, bit my tongue, and drove off.

After the ten-hour drive, we finally pulled into the driveway, and I thought I might be sick. What looked like a gorgeous cottage in the pictures looked instead like something out of the movie *Friday the 13th*. The roof needed work, the porch was almost falling apart, and the lawn was a mess. The ocean sat on one side and a state park sat on the other. Houses were scarce, and if something bad were to happen, nobody would hear us scream. I obviously have watched too many movies and worked too many police cases. My mind may have wandered into a deep and dark place. How was I going to come up with a thousand dollars to find other lodging? I couldn't let the family prove me wrong. I heard Alto tell me to trust him and to just go in, and we did, although we left the luggage in the car and first looked around. The moment we stepped into the home, we were pleasantly surprised. It was charming, clean, and bright. I sighed with relief and air-hugged Alto.

Within the hour, we found ourselves running down to the beach, but were stopped in our tracks. Moonstones. The beach was covered in moonstones, which are gemstones said to have magical powers. There were all different colors and sizes. We all giggled and began gathering the moonstones in jars that we brought for shells. The stones were about the size of a penny and gave off a mysterious shimmer. In earlier times, many believed that the ocean would gift the shore these stones during the crescent and waning phases of the moon. We felt as if we had discovered a long-lost secret, our personal treasures.

I tell my clients to ask for signs from their angels and guides and to be specific when asking. Someone's sign may be a rainbow, an orange poppy, or even a turtle. Mine happens to be the word "BELIEVE." The evening of our first night there, I sat on the crooked wooden deck, rocking in the white wicker chair, and contemplated life. I disliked my real job with a passion, even with a promotion. Although I was grateful for the opportunity, and the large office that was specially constructed for me, I knew that wasn't my calling. It wasn't what I was supposed to be doing. I knew it. I felt it. Tears filled my eyes as I thought of returning to the job that I so disliked, so I asked my angels and guides to give me a sign. I was miserable, but I didn't know how I was just supposed to up and quit my job—a job that offered future security with a pension, medical benefits, paid vacation days, and a steady paycheck. As I sniffled back the sobs, I felt someone watching me and looked up to see a hummingbird floating right in front of me. For at least ten seconds, we both looked into one another's eyes. He floated backwards and then flew back into the woods. It felt so … spiritual.

The second day of vacation we decided to venture into Baltimore. The kids were cranky, Chuck was cranky, and well, I was cranky because they were. Also, I was still contemplating how to make changes in my life and my boss was continually calling, which wasn't helping the rest-and-relaxation part of vacation. As we turned the corner off the freeway, Chuck pointed out a billboard. It said "BELIEVE." The kids frantically began pointing all over. Trash cans, window signs, the baseball stadium … everywhere the word "BELIEVE" was written. It just so happened to be the slogan for Baltimore that year—how coincidental was that? I stood there and wept in the streets of Baltimore. Moonstones and now my sign. So what did it all mean?

I had some soul searching to do in order to figure out exactly what it all meant. What I did know was that I didn't want to sit in my new office. I wanted to sit on a beach with my laptop and type out award-winning stories by day and do readings and lectures at night. Too much to ask? I didn't think so.

Was it a coincidence that my finger landed where it did? Was it a coincidence that "BELIEVE" was Baltimore's theme that year? I didn't think so. I believed that by finally trusting my intuition, I held the key to unlock new doorways and opportunities. And that I was going to have to release my past in order to fully move forward.

As if right on cue to helping in the release, I came home from my trip to find an email from Jason's past mistress that helped in my recovery.

*Dear Kristy,*

*I'll start with the most important thing, and that is my sincere apology to you. I played a big part in turning your life and the lives of your innocent children upside down, and I truly regret that. There is no explanation for my behavior—I don't even understand it myself. Is it possible to claim temporary insanity for a year of horribly bad decisions? I don't know who that selfish and heartless person was, but I hate her and know that I will never be that person again. That wasn't me. I am so sorry for all of the misery I caused you. Words cannot express how ashamed I am of that very low point in my life. If it were possible, I'd go back and take a completely different path— one that didn't involve one Jason. I don't expect forgiveness from you, but I wanted you to know that I am truly sorry.*

It took me a moment to let it all settle. I thought I had stuffed that ghost of the past in a locked trunk, but all the feelings of embarrassment and fear came flooding back. Chuck kept asking me to marry him over and over, and I kept telling him that the timing was wrong. In retrospect, I was petrified of being a failure as a wife.

I ended up responding:

*To be perfectly honest, I came very close to hitting "delete" before I even read your email, but I am glad that I didn't. I thank you for the apology. I am still a bit numb out of surprise.*

*As I look back over the whole ordeal, which I really rarely do, I cannot lie and say that everything was wonderful after the divorce. Financially, I suffered a lot (and continue to), but money can always be created. It was my children who I believe suffered the most. In the end, they are just fine. I firmly believe that God works in mysterious ways and in actuality the divorce was probably the best thing for all of us. After the divorce, my mother became quite ill, and my move enabled me to be near during her last year of life. Also, I am now in a wonderful relationship with a man; a relationship that can't be wholly explained other than plain kismet. And a relationship that I never had with Jason or ever thought could be possible.*

*I wish you nothing but love and happiness.*

The closure that I received from that part of my life helped me to not just close the chapter from the past, but write "The End" and start writing a new and even better book of my life.

# twenty-five

# Married to a Medium

And then I said yes. Third time is a charm, right?

Our wedding was Saturday, October 14, 2006, overlooking a moonlit lake, with our children and immediate family. It was intimate, sweet, and funny all wrapped up in the warmth of love (and we needed it—it was COLD!!).

The day started out like a *Cheaper by the Dozen* movie with our Husky puppy eating three month's worth of blood pressure medication and one of Chuck's daughters spraining her ankle playing volleyball and having to visit Urgent Care. By the afternoon, we were begging the kids to just stay seated and do nothing but look at the television before another disaster struck.

Having not had a rehearsal, to say that we bumbled our way through is putting it lightly. Chuck stood staring at me in the doorway, forgetting his prompt to actually come get me until the wedding planner hissed at him, setting him into motion. At one point during the ceremony, Chuck turned around and apologized to everybody for our comical errors, which got a chuckle out of the minister and our guests. It took mere moments before we were pronounced "Man and Wife" and he was given the A-OK to kiss me, which didn't seem good enough to the minister because he told him that he knew he could do better—making all of the kids hide their eyes. Chuck, the kids, and I did a lovely sand ceremony in which everybody was represented by a different color of sand; now we have a beautiful vase filled with the sand as a remembrance, showing that although we are individuals, we are now a family. I admit it...I did cry, and even though Chuck will deny it, his eyes started watering too (and it wasn't from the cold wind coming off the lake). Although everything was very "untraditional," our music had special meaning for us. Our guests walked down to the Carpenters' "We've Only Just Begun," followed by Chuck and I walking down to "At Last" by Etta James, and the processional was in memory of my mom, a Frank Sinatra fan: "The Best Is Yet to Come."

---

Before I married my first husband, I fell in love with a man who I will call Ryan. Ryan would've been the man of my dreams except for the fact that I was already in love with the man of my dreams. The timing was ironic to say the least. Or was it divine?

Still quite young and not quite certain what I wanted to do with my life, I signed up to work with a temporary agency just to get my feet wet in several different industries. The agency matched me with a construction management firm at Detroit Metropolitan Airport that was managing several projects, including a runway expansion and a new parking lot structure. The company loved me so much that they ended up hiring me, and I was transferred to a public school (which, over ten years, later would go on to to hire me full time in another capacity). Although I didn't love it, I was good at the administrative work. When that project ended, I was transferred to a job site quite far from my home. I balked immediately and begged for another assignment, but they claimed that nothing else was available, and since I was nineteen years old and getting paid quite a lot of money, I wasn't about to argue the fact.

My supervisor at this job location was a bit of an odd duck. He didn't like women, and yet he had bipolar qualities where he could pull on one mask for the superiors and then immediately take it off when they were out of earshot. It was so hard to figure out who he would be one day to the next that I finally put aside my shyness and scheduled a conference with my supervisor's supervisor. Since the project owners liked me, my company decided that, instead of transferring me, they would add another employee to our office as a buffer. This buffer's name was Ryan.

Ryan was completing his college education and had high aspirations of climbing the ladder of the construction-management business. Without my help, he immediately saw our boss's instability and went into protective mode.

We lunched together daily and began to bond as friends, and then, as time went on, feelings grew stronger. I didn't cheat. It just wasn't me. However, there were times that I wondered if the man (or woman) upstairs had played a cruel joke on me. Ryan and I had a connection that could only be called timeless. He knew what I was thinking before I said it, so words never had to be spoken. He had a girlfriend and I was set to marry my high school sweetheart, so there was no way that anything could ever progress—neither of us wanting to cause issues within our other relationships. Both of us being mature and realistic, he ended up transferring so that we both could be put out of our misery. Out of sight, out of mind.

A year later, with a wedding ring on my finger, I was asked to do work at another job site, and there was Ryan. I was excited to see him again, but he acted cold and aloof toward me, which left me feeling heartbroken all over again. I thought that perhaps we could still be friends, but something had changed within him and, since I didn't deal well with conflict, I suppressed my hurt feelings and did what I was supposed to do: work. That was until I couldn't take it anymore and outright left the construction management firm for an entirely different type of job. I never heard from Ryan again... *until a few nights before my wedding to Chuck.*

It didn't come in the form of a phone call, an email, or a letter. Instead, I was awoken from a dead sleep by a gentle nudging, only to find Ryan sitting next to me in bed. He smiled at me, his green eyes sparkling. He looked the same except for some speckles of gray in his raven-black hair. Even his stature was the same: thin and gangly. What was different, however, was that he was in spirit and not flesh and blood. He told me that he had passed away and that he wanted me to know. He went on to say that I always meant a lot to him and that he never forgot me. He explained how jealous he had been that I had married and how it was easier to ignore than to understand. He laughed and told me that he approved of my current marriage because Chuck reminded him a lot of himself. He said that he would be watching over me to make sure I stayed out of trouble. He grinned as he teased me. He said that everything happens for a reason and, looking me in my eyes, asked me how I would've felt if we had gotten together and had kids. The kids would've been left without a father. Always reasons, never random. The tears were stuck in my throat and although I claim endless times that I can talk to a tree stump, I was at a loss of words.

"I know you've been hurt. I helped find Chuck for you," Ryan said and grabbed my hand. "Remember the Madonna song."

And then he disappeared.

I was left shaken and emotional, replaying not only the visit, but also our past. There are always reasons as to why things happen in our life. It is never random, and it is never to punish us. And so perhaps the reason why Ryan and I weren't supposed to be together was because I wasn't supposed to lose a husband and (perhaps) a father to my children, or maybe there was another reason that I didn't know and wasn't supposed to.

The Madonna comment stumped me. Ryan was a Nine Inch Nails type of guy, definitely not a card-carrying Madonna fan club member. Clarity came the following day, though, when I was still pondering the meaning and turned the car on only to have Madonna's "Lucky Star" blaring back at me on the radio. Ryan always told me that I was his lucky star and that one day I would make it big and shine for others.

The messages are never random. Our life is never random. There are always reasons behind how things play out.

Rest in peace, Ryan.

# twenty-six

# *An Epiphany*

I was still working at the metaphysical center, but wasn't feeling satisfied. Although the center was supposed to be all about love and light, the drama and cattiness between the readers was hate and dark. On several occasions, I would go into the center only to see my name erased and no clients on my schedule. I spoke to the owner, but the person who had it out for me was his own daughter. I would simply sit there for several hours hoping for a walk-in, and then go home with only five to twenty dollars.

I worked every Thursday because the kids were at their father's house, so I would run home after my day job, grab something to eat and change my clothes, and then run to the center for three hours and then go home and crash. But when Thursday came and I checked my schedule, I once again saw that my name had been erased and there were no clients noted. I was furious and just about ready to walk out when a middle-aged man came in and grabbed me in a hug. I had read for him several times, but not recently.

"Kristy! I called earlier to see if you were in, but I was told you wouldn't be. I took a chance and drove by to see, just in case you came in."

I clenched my teeth, angry once more that my schedule was being sabotaged and the clients lied to. Not only was I not getting the business, the center wasn't getting the business.

I took him to my office, which I was now sharing with another reader, when I noticed that he was dressed in pajamas, and the red flags started to go off.

"Phil, are you okay?" I asked, knowing the answer, but stalling in order to bring in my guides and his guides so that I could get a better grasp on his energy.

"No, Kristy, I am not. I have nothing left to live for. I have a gun in my car and if you weren't here I was going to go to the park to shoot myself."

Trying to hold it together as best I could, I begged for anybody from the Other Side to come through with a message. Thankfully, his wife, who had passed away from cancer two years earlier, came through.

"Phil, if you do this, you won't be able to be with me," she said, and I shared the message.

She begged me to get him help. I explained to him that committing suicide wasn't the answer and that he would have to learn lessons when he crossed, if he crossed, and wouldn't be able to be with his loved ones for who knows how long. His mental state wasn't ready to grasp it, but he allowed me to call the police to get him some help.

I was grateful for being at the right place at the right time and potentially saving a life, but I was so angry that because of the snarkiness there could have been a whole other ending. I wrote out my resignation right then and there and decided to do readings out of my home. If I attracted clients, great; if I didn't, great. I decided that I wouldn't advertise, but would create a website and let word of mouth be my billboard.

Doing readings out of my home was interesting. The dining room table became my office as the dogs, cat, Chuck, and the kids would go downstairs until they heard me pound on the floor, signaling that I was done. I had a steady stream of customers who came every Saturday to hear what their guides had to say, and what loved ones came through on the Other Side. I had an eclectic group of clients, everybody from lawyers to celebrities to moms to mobsters' wives. Surprisingly, the gender breakdown was about fifty-fifty. One client who came to me was named Gayle.

She was a pretty lady with short, bright red hair and blue eyes. I knew that she was looking for her son, but the first visitor who came with a message was a male who claimed to have been her mentor. She was a bit confused until she realized that it wasn't about her day job, but her side job. During the day she was a paraprofessional, working with special education children, but at nighttime she was a hypnotherapist. It was then her son, Brent, came through.

Only in his thirties, he'd died a year earlier from a heart condition and felt awful leaving his mom with a mess, emotionally and financially. Gayle kept a poker face throughout the session, and I didn't think she enjoyed it at all, although she gave me her business card and a hug on the way out.

A few hours after Gayle's appointment, I rushed over to a hotel conference room that was overflowing, standing room only, with over seven hundred people patiently awaiting the arrival of an author who also claimed to be a involved in metaphysics. For one (free) night, two hours of time, he would show everybody else how to be successful in business and in life. Now, I didn't just fall off the turnip truck last week, so I knew (or did I know?) there was a catch. As always, "free" rarely means really free, does it? But I had followed him for a while through websites, blogs, and books, and since we are in similar fields, I wanted to see what he had to say.

Sitting in the second row, I mingled with two women and a man who were there alone and we began sharing our stories. They were in dead-end jobs, dead-end relationships, and felt as if there was no other way to escape the routine of life. Were they destined to be miserable? Obviously they didn't feel that way since they were taking a step in a new direction to hear alternatives. Seven hundred people had similar stories. I explained to them my enlightening year and reassured them that if I could change my life into one of purpose, they too could do it, whether they wanted to go back to school, find a better job, or open their own business—if I could do it, anybody could. Forty minutes or so later, when the author was introduced by a scripted, robotic-type woman, I knew that I was in trouble. Greeted by a standing ovation, the man ran out on stage and began sharing a summary of his life and how he got to where he was. We then had to go through several public exercises, which were truly uncomfortable for me, but I played along and ran around the room hugging complete strangers just as instructed. At one point, I found myself next to the author himself, and he shared a hug with me and it was then... it was then that I had a psychic epiphany that this man, a well-respected man in the metaphysical community, was a charlatan. I saw badges around him, my sign that he would be exposed, causing his reputation and everything he'd built to come crashing down. After we found our seats, the presenter sat down on a stool in the center of the stage and asked for questions from the audience.

And they did ask, but were very hesitant—to tell you the truth, not only did I not blame them, I felt embarrassed for them because one by one he judgmentally chewed them up. Did they deserve it? Not the way he did it. He went on to explain manifesting secrets, which really aren't a secret, and detailed life-changing results from people who had gone to his conferences. He bragged about the people he hangs with and yet, in the same breath, explained how he learned from his arrogance in younger years and knew he had to dismiss it. Did he really learn? Two hours sped by and then I waited with apprehension for the catch. And it came and it came quick. Buy this, and buy that, and if you don't, you won't ever be successful. As I sat there, I did some quick figures in my head at how much he made off of his "free" seminar, and it went past the half million dollar mark as the lines lengthened to secure their future. The threats continued to echo as I made my way to the exit empty-handed. Or sort of. I left with an epiphany.

One of the girls who'd sat next to me began to get emotional because she was a single mom who couldn't afford to fly to the various workshop locations. The other girl, a college student who had lost her job at Ford Motor Company, couldn't afford the expensive CD and book package, and the man just felt deflated. They looked heartbroken. I was sick, knowing that the author was playing with people's minds. He was creating the thought that you are a loser if you didn't do this—the very thing that he was telling the audience to erase from their psyche! He was playing the game and he was playing it well. I wrote on my notepad some websites that they could go to, YouTube videos that would help, and handed them my card and class schedule. I wasn't pimping myself out and saying I was better, but I was showing them that there are options. A whole lot of options, and it didn't involve sitting in a stuffy conference room for two days while you gave over thousands of dollars to a multimillionaire as he laughed all the way to the bank in his private cabana in the Caribbean, or Hawaii, or wherever he had gotten that great tan.

That earlier hug that I mentioned made me realize many things. It made me realize that I am knowledgeable. That I am ethical and honest and that I am talented and funny and that I was filled with love. I hugged this man and all I felt was nothing—nothing but an empty shell of someone enjoying his riches and someone not truly living. Who said nothing was free? I received an epiphany.

Two days after my epiphany and my appointment with Gayle, I had one client on my schedule. The kids were at their father's house, and Chuck was staying at his mom's house for the night to help her with errands, so I was excited to do this one appointment and then spend time some time relaxing. Working out of my home was irritating because I had to keep it continually clean. While wiping down the kitchen counters, I heard a soft knock that resulted in rapid knocks. I opened my door to see a handsome young man standing there. He introduced himself as Todd, my next appointment, and the man I'd been seated next to at the conference. I noticed his gray eyes and his brown tousled hair as he sat down across from me. Beginning the session as I always do, I asked him to take a deep breath in and out and state his full name. As he completed his instructions, I closed my eyes and wrapped myself in his energy. The vision came rapidly, as if someone was changing the television channel, each one as dismal and as cloudy as the color of his eyes. Typically, I don't ask for information, but my guides insisted that I do this time.

"Todd, my guides are telling me that you have something to give me. Can I see it?"

Todd looked at me, stunned. "How did you ... ?"

I gently smiled and reminded him that I was a psychic.

He slowly stood up and reached in his back jean pocket and handed me a crumpled up piece of paper.

Unfolding the yellow-lined paper, I drew in my breath, afraid that the visions that I saw seconds before were spot on. The note read, "I have lost everything and don't feel as if I have anything to live for. I am sorry if I caused you any pain. I wish I could see a way out." Below the note were names and phone numbers of loved ones that were to be contacted. It was obvious that it was a suicide note and I instantly went into an adrenaline rush. Did he have a gun with him? My guides told me no. Was he really suicidal? My guides told me that he was and that it was serious, but he wanted to live more than die. He was seeking help. Answers. The reason for his appointment.

The appointment lasted almost two hours as I explained to him what I saw for him in the future if he sought help. I talked about what it was like for those who commit suicide and how the struggles don't just go away, that they are merely moved from this world to the other. At the end of the appointment, we had a plan of action, a call in to his doctor, and his family on the way to meet him. It would all be okay.

You don't have to be a psychic to recognize the signs of depression or suicide. In this economy, more and more people are losing hope. By being aware of your loved ones, what they are saying, and their moods, you can make a difference. I was at the conference for a specific reason: to offer direction to a suicidal man.

In each moment of our lives, we receive messages that can be life changing. It doesn't have to be an earth-shattering experience, but can happen even in the quiet on an autumn walk. Don't always look for the flashing neon signs, because epiphanies seldom come that way. It could simply be the deer that you encounter in the woods that stops and looks you in the eye before gallantly running away. Or the child who runs up to you with a simple hug. Or a boss who pats you on the back and offers you words of encouragement. But the biggest question of them all is "What lessons will you learn with your epiphanies?"

After I told Chuck about the appointment, I realized that I needed an office outside of the house, and I picked up Gayle's business card. It took a few days before I got the guts to call her, only to talk to her answering machine.

"Hi Gayle, this is Kristy, the psychic medium that you saw a week ago, and I was talking to my spirit guides—well, they said that I should call you to see if you might want to share an office."

I wasn't even convinced she'd enjoyed her reading, so I was taking a chance, but my guides assured me it would change my life, whatever that meant. A few hours later she called me back and invited me to her office to talk. Our talk ended up being several hours long, where we laughed, cried, and talked about her son and her past, my mom and my past. I could sense both her son and my mom just watching us, and it was then that I realized that someone schemed something on the Other Side. The next week I signed the lease for my office in the same building as Gayle. I didn't have a clue how I was going to pay for it, but I threw caution to the wind.

Several months later I was taking a shower when I sensed someone else in the bathroom with me. There was Gayle's son, Brent. I screeched and he chuckled. After I shared my shower encounter with Gayle, she just laughed and said that would be just like her son.

# twenty-seven

# Full Circle

After my mom crossed over, Chuck, the kids, and I took my dad to lunch to discuss buying a home together. Although my father was physically able to take care of himself and his home, he was emotionally depleted. And we were too. We were taking care of our household and then going over and doing his chores. It was becoming too much.

We put both of our homes up for sale and waited. And waited. And waited. This was right before the economy tanked and the real estate market was already beginning to slow down. We were also our own competition. Our homes were only a mile apart, so anybody looking at my home was going to look at his, too. For anybody who has had their home on the market, attempting to keep it as immaculate as possible at all times is incredibly stressful. After a few months, we just took the homes off the market.

I was getting ready for lunch when my cell phone rang, and I saw that it was my father. My heart skipped a beat. He only called me with bad news.

"Dad? Are you all right?" I answered. I walked out of my office, waved to the secretary, and headed to my car.

"How soon can we move?"

Had he hit his head or had another heart attack? Our houses weren't even up for sale.

"Did you win the lottery?" I joked, secretly hoping that he did, but knowing that he rarely bought a ticket made me think that wasn't going to happen.

"Kind of." I could hear him grinning. "A lady knocked on my door this morning and is interested in my home. She has a home in Livonia that is too large, and mine is just right. We're going to trade houses. She's going to take my home, and we're going to take hers."

"Dad, don't sign anything yet. We don't even know what her house looks like!"

He sighed and I knew that he was rolling his eyes at me. "Kristy, I wouldn't sign anything. We're going to go over there when you get off of work."

The house wasn't my dream home, but it was in a good neighborhood and was twice as large as either of ours. A few months later we moved into the gray and white brick ranch home and combined our households. I knew that sooner rather than later I would have to speak to my dad about my side job, but I was afraid of his reaction. Most days (and nights) he had some evangelical screaming on the television and was reading his Bible. I didn't want him disappointed in me.

A local newspaper did a story on me entitled "The Ghost Hunter." It spoke of the different police cases I was working on, and spelled out my abilities. Although I asked that they only use my first name, I hid the paper from my dad, afraid that he would put two and two together before I got the confidence to confess. I couldn't, however, hide the paper from everybody. The morning after the story came out I saw a group of coworkers in the coffee room reading the article. I ducked out of the way, but one lady caught me.

"Is this about you, Kristy?"

I glanced at the paper as if I had never seen it. "Now when would I find the time to do all that?" I sputtered.

Not long after that article, another article came out in a larger publication, and I once again pulled the section out before giving the paper to my father. I realized that it was ridiculous. I was thirty-something years old and hiding things from my dad, but it was my mom who decided to help me with the confession.

I think it is important to have dinner together at least once a week. One evening as we sat down at the table for dinner, we were chatting about the day when a loaf of bread flew from the kitchen into the dining area and landed smack dab on the middle of the table. We didn't know whether to scream, laugh, or run. I saw my mom standing there in spirit, mischievously grinning, but I didn't have to say a thing. It was my dad who asked if I thought mom had thrown the bread at him. I nodded and confessed to seeing her, and seeing others. He still looked at me like I was nuts, but the weight came off my shoulders nonetheless, and I slowly began to share my stories of my job with him, and I stopped hiding the news articles or unplugging the cable when a television show featuring me was on.

It was an enlightening visit from my dad's sister, Cathy, that helped to shed some light on my gift.

"Kristy, it's so wonderful that you're a medium. You must have gotten the gift from our side of the family."

I looked at her, confused.

"Your grandmother's father was sought out by women as soon as their pregnancies were confirmed by the doctor. Grandpa could look at them and instantly tell them the sex of the baby."

"Really?" I said, giving my dad a sideways look at this new revelation.

"And your great-grandma, well, she was a tea-leaf reader."

My dad continued to avoid my gaze.

The conversation continued on to reveal that my grandmother wasn't a fan of her parents' gifts, so could she have perhaps seen the same gift within me, inspiring her hatred?

With my great-grandparents on my dad's side and my grandfather on my mom's side all being gifted, I laughed, thinking that I was doubly cursed.

Cathy went on to tell me of some more family history, which involved a relation to a famous witch. A genealogist by hobby, Cathy found out that we were direct descendants to Mary Bliss Parsons, a rumored witch during the Salem Witch Trials.

Witches were feared for their ability to affect natural phenomena, but many of the times disgruntled neighbors or town folk used the witch label to point fingers at those they were angry at or jealous of. If an execution took place, it helped eliminate their case of envy. So it was never determined if Mary was truly a witch, or just a prominent lady who existed in the 1600s and wasn't liked. I like to think of her as possibly both.

# twenty-eight

# Starting Over

I had so much on my plate, missed my mom like mad, had received a promotion at work, and was petrified of messing up another marriage. Driving to work one morning, the anxiety and pressure built up so much that I burst into tears as I maneuvered my way through the winding road that I had driven for over six years. I heard someone clear their throat next to me, and almost ran off the road when I saw an African American man sitting in the passenger seat, his feet lounging on the console.

"Who are you?" I gasped.

"Your new guide. I'm Marvin, but I prefer Marv."

"What? Where's Alto? And Tallie?"

"They're still around, but there are some major life changes happening and I'm just the man to help."

Marv had a smooth way of talking, almost melodic. I felt comfortable around him, even though we just met. That is the thing about a guide; you are gifted them, to help as a best friend would, only with clearer objectives.

Just as I went to ask him more questions, I looked over to see that he had disappeared. It would have to wait.

I plopped into my seat at 8:00 a.m. to start my day.

Sitting in my brand-new office with my brand-new furniture and brand-new computer, I closed my eyes and tried to wish away the tears. I worked with strong people, and I knew that tears wouldn't be acceptable. I begged my guides for an answer. I had accepted a promotion in my "real" job in hopes that it would make me happy, but it was doing the opposite. I was miserable. Before I could feel sorry for myself anymore, my phone rang and I was off and working. The clock read 4:00 p.m. when I clutched my hand to my chest. I ached and I ached horribly. I asked my guides if I was having a heart attack and received the all clear, but I knew something was wrong. As if on cue, my boss walked by and noticed that I was turning a nice shade of khaki green. She promptly asked me if I wanted an ambulance, and although there were signs of something serious, I told her I would just go to my doctor. I grabbed my purse and drove across the street to see what in the world was going on. That was the last day I would ever step foot in that office again—over five years ago now.

My anxiety and panic over being miserable had manifested illness within me. The diagnoses ranged from mononucleosis to chronic fatigue and finally to fibromyalgia. Here

I was teaching my clients to take care of themselves, and I was doing just the opposite. I panicked going back to work, and I panicked not going back to work—what was I going to do? After several months of lying on the couch in exhaustion from the illness, I was festering in a pool of anger at a disability company that sat outside my house, spying on me. I was angry at my workplace for not believing that I was actually ill. I was angry at myself for allowing myself to get so stressed, and so sick, and for not listening to my intuition and my guides. Every time I thought I was getting well enough to return to my position, I got ill again. I sat for over five hours in my doctor's office, my husband curled up next to me on the exam table, holding me as I sobbed when the doctor asked me what I thought I could do to get well. The blood tests were there in black and white, evidence that showed that I was sick—it wasn't all in my head—but the disability company refused to pay me, stating that it was anxiety and nothing more. And my workplace wanted an answer. I finally looked up at the doctor and my husband and said, "I think the prescription is resignation." They both nodded in agreement. It was like a weight had fallen off my shoulders as soon as I made the announcement. Explaining to my family that I was going to quit my job, and then giving my formal resignation, was difficult and frightening. I grew up in a household where you pack a brown bag lunch and work for 8.5 hours and come home. Nothing less, nothing more.

Rosanne Cash is quoted as saying that "the key to change is to let go of fear." Fear is what kept me rooted longer than

I should have been. As I let go of my fears and embraced growth, the change allowed me to flourish. I knew that I had a calling and that I couldn't do it being stuck in an office that I hated, a job that wasn't a good fit. All I was doing was causing resistance, which was the reason behind my illnesses.

It was a tug of war with my destiny.

# twenty-nine

# *Embracing My Fears*

I love the beauty of birds—each species unique in their markings, colors, and habits. I have always admired them from afar for their freedom—wings spread without a known care in the world. However, I never had any up-close interaction until I took a trip to a pet store the day before I was to be hospitalized for a blood transfusion and then have a full hysterectomy.

I've never claimed to be a pet psychic, and in fact I still don't. I had inherited my mom's fears of birds, but during my time off of work, I would venture to the local pet store. It seemed to help with my stress and anxiety. I would play with the puppies and the kittens, but it was one certain pet shop parakeet that grabbed my eye.

As I went up to his cage, he bounced right up to me and began to *telepathically* speak to me. He told me to call him Sarge and that he had been a military fighter in the Army. It was my third visit to his cage when I told my husband that the bird was talking to me.

"You have to buy him," Chuck urged.

Chuck had been around birds all his life, so he didn't understand my fear of its flapping wings, pointy beak, and intimidating claws. Not only was I frightened, I had no time, or money, to take care of a bird. And then add in that the bird could actually talk to me! I would never get any rest!

The joke would later be on me.

Ever since the mononucleosis, my blood count kept dipping dangerously low, and I was having awful stomach pains that sent me to the emergency room several times. During one emergency room visit, I was lying in the bed awaiting tests as the doctors were sure that I had appendicitis when a spirit of an older black lady stood next to my bedside. She didn't say anything, just stared at me. I wasn't even certain how to react, but after about ten minutes of her just staring at me, I started a conversation. I thought that if a doctor or nurse caught me talking to the air that I could at least blame the painkillers they had given me.

"Have you ever heard that it wasn't polite to stare?" I told her.

She broke down in tears.

"I'm sorry, I'm sorry! I was trying to be funny. Did you pass away here?"

"I don't think so," she sniffled, wiping her tears with the back of her hand.

I was confused. If she didn't pass away there, why was she hanging around a hospital?

Before I could ask any more questions, a nurse came in.

"Ask her who is behind the curtain," the lady said.

I giggled, wanting to tell her it might be the Wizard of Oz, but then realized I was being rude and giddy off of the drugs.

"Nurse, can you tell me who is in the next room to me?"

"Why do you ask?"

"Is there possibly a deceased lady of about seventy-something lying there?"

She moved the curtain aside, pushed her head in and out quickly, looked at me strangely, and ran out of my room. It wasn't long before I heard several people in the room next to me.

The spirit bent over and gave me a kiss. "By the way, my name is Delores in case anyone asks," she said, and then she walked back over to her room.

The nurse came back, her eyes large and questioning. "How did you know that there was a deceased patient?"

"Because she told me she was there," I replied simply. "And by the way, her name is Delores."

It was true. That morning Delores had passed away in the cab on the way to the hospital. She didn't have any identification on her, and they left her there in hopes that someone would come and ID her. Then, after a shift change, she was all but forgotten. Until I came along.

They determined that I didn't have appendicitis and sent me home with pain pills. That week my doctor decided that they would have to do a full hysterectomy, but first do a blood transfusion. I was scared, but had high hopes that it would help solve the mounting medical ailments.

The morning started off early with dropping the kids off at school and then making my way to the hospital for my blood transfusion. I was surprised to check in and be told that my room was ready. They walked me to a regular room and told my husband and me to make ourselves at home. Because I was wearing comfy clothes, they didn't even make me change into a gown! So I lay in bed with some nice warm blankets and the hubby settled down in the recliner and they started the IV. It took a while for them to bring me my blood because they hadn't done a cross check on my blood and that took an extra hour. I was a nervous wreck about the blood going in me, but the nurses were being so sweet about everything. What made me even more nervous was that I could not only taste the saline from the IV, I could then taste the blood and actually feel it as it circulated in my body (including in my eye veins). What was even more scary for all of us was that my blood was making odd noises...almost an electric/vibration type noise that had us all staring at one another. They said they'd never heard of anything like it. We all blamed it on the empath in me because a normal person should not be that in tune to the body and the circulatory system. When I explained to the medical practitioners how I felt it move, they said it was exactly the way the anatomy ran (and sorry...I never took that class!). Even though I didn't know what was going on, I would later discover that the vibrations came about because my body was out of sync, and much like maintenance working on an elevator, and lubricating its moving parts by sending it to the top floor, the transfusion was doing the same by realigning my chakras and cleansing my aura.

Because I was on clear liquids that day, the nurses were nice about bringing me anything that went under that category...and even made me some iced tea. I finally fell asleep around 1:00 p.m., but awoke to the spirit of a young woman standing over me. I looked to see if my husband saw her, but he was snoring away. She said her name was Tanya and that she had just recently passed, but that she didn't have family that much cared. I felt so bad for her, but she didn't want to have anything to do with going to the light and continued to sit with me throughout my hospital stay. She kept stroking my right hand and saying that we would've been friends if she had known me. I thought that was sweet, and it made me feel even worse.

The nurse came in with a second pint of blood, which took forever, and then tried to convince me to stay the night as my hysterectomy was scheduled first thing the next morning. However, between the ghosts, the uncomfortable bed, my fear of hospitals (see ghost comment), and my desire to take a hot bath, I opted to go home and just go back there at 6:30 in the morning.

The hysterectomy was pretty much like my C-section, only I wasn't rewarded with a baby to hold. I became allergic to everything and blamed the blood transfusion, which was only met with smirks from the hospital staff as they explained that it didn't work that way. Well, I never had allergies before, I would huff. I couldn't sleep. I itched, and I hurt.

I finally dozed off after all my visitors had left, only to hear the television go on. I snapped my eyes open and saw the spirit of my mom sitting in the chair next to me.

"Mom?" I asked.

"Dear, just go back to sleep. I'm just going to catch up on my soaps."

I looked at the television and sure enough, *All My Children* was playing. I didn't want to sleep, I wanted to visit. It had been almost a year since she had crossed over, but she stroked my hair and I fell into a peaceful sleep.

That night I was agitated and teary after the interaction with Mom, so they finally gave me some sleeping medication. I remember waking up and seeing my family standing there and Chuck telling me to follow him. So, I somehow got up, put clothes over my IV, and began dragging my pole with me. The family led me to a window and told me to jump, that I would be caught. I snapped out of the haze to realize that I didn't know where I was, what room I was supposed to be in, or what my name was. A nurse found me sobbing and took me back to my room where they kept guard on me all night. No sleeping medication for me!

After several days, I was granted a release from the hospital and was thrilled to be home and in my own bed. I was on the phone with a friend when my son rushed into the house. Normally very polite, he urgently pulled at my sleeve, jumping from one foot to the next. Excusing myself from the conversation, I asked him what the deal was. In a dress-up Army hat was a baby robin. I first squawked myself and then panicked. What do I do with a baby bird? Thankfully it wasn't long before my husband came home from work and Dr. Doolittle went to work on showing me how to feed and care for her, a girl we promptly named Lillith (Lily). We created a makeshift nest in a laundry basket and hand-fed her fruit and blueberry muffins. She refused to leave, so we spent time teaching her how to peck, and we fell in love. She would fly to and nuzzle the dogs' faces and fall asleep on our shoulders. We figured that we would keep her until her tail feathers came in, and continued to take her for dry runs.

Since I tend to find a spiritual message in almost everything that happens in life, I meditated on it and was told to search out what a Robin totem meant. The name Robin actually means *Bright Fame*, but as for the totem, a Robin totem will stimulate new growth in all areas of life. So it all made complete sense, at least to the two people who were getting the most out of our lovely Lillith—my husband and me.

We had hopes that Lily would understand that we had learned the lesson and join her family again—knowing that she would always have us to come to if she needed a blueberry muffin.

I went to lie down for my nap when my husband came running into the bedroom, crying and holding Lillith. She had died in his hands.

That little bird taught me so much about facing my fears and examining my life in order to overcome. Even little fragments of messages can communicate a lot. And my fear of birds? What fear?

I was raised with the theology that animals don't go to heaven because they have no soul. Anytime we studied that part of the Bible in school, I would shake my head in disbelief. It just couldn't be true, I thought.

I grew up around a pet, and it was after the kids' dad left that I found myself caring for Conan, a Great Pyrenees who was a gentle giant. A hundred and fifty pounds of white fluff, he was great with the kids, and a wonderful protector for me being a single mom. I began to notice that he was having issues with his back legs and took him to the vetrinarian where they gave us the bad news—he had heartworm and probably wouldn't make it. Even though I faithfully gave him his medication, the doctor thought that because he was so large, his given dose hadn't been enough to prevent it. I was devastated and even more saddened to tell the kids that their faithful pet was going to die. The doctor told me to bring him in when I was ready, or when Conan was ready.

After a few months, I knew that it was time. The car ride to the clinic, just Conan and myself, was heart wrenching. I sobbed and tried to see the road through my waterworks.

Sitting in the small room with Conan lying in my lap, his large brown eyes looking into mine with a knowing, I hugged his head and broke down again. The veterinarian, a kindhearted man, sat on the floor next to us and slowly and quietly helped Conan find his peace. I left with his collar and leash and a heavy heart.

A year or so afterwards, Connor kept tripping. He was five years old and I was worried that he had a medical issue, or was just extremely clumsy.

"What's going on, Connor?" I asked, exasperated.

"It's Conan," he answered easily.

I gave him that look that says to tell the truth.

"It is Conan, Mom! It is. He keeps walking in front of me."

I let it go because Connor rarely if ever lied.

"Mom! Mom!"

It was a couple days after the Conan talk when I heard Connor yelling at me from his bedroom. I raced from the kitchen to his room, where I found him crying and petting the air. There, in spirit, was Conan. Not only did I see him, there was no denying it. Connor's bed was weighed down the way only a one-hundred-fifty-pound dog could do to a youth bed. Just as soon as he appeared, he slowly disappeared and the mattress took back its shape.

We never saw Conan again, and Connor's tripping stopped.

Conan gave us his final goodbye before his final stay in heaven. And yes, I do believe that animals go to heaven. How couldn't they, with as much as joy and love as they give us here on earth?

# thirty

# *Follow Your Path*

Success surely doesn't happen overnight. It's a journey that encounters many obstacles, mistakes, and even some wounds. Whether it is finding your soul mate, a fulfilling relationship, or a satisfying job, you don't wake up one day with knowledge of exactly what you want out of life and find yourself saying, "If only…"

Among the array of reasons one doesn't succeed, the main one is fear. Fear of failure (or sometimes fear of success) creates a chaos of overthinking and overanalyzing, which roots the vibration into what I call the bottom-feeder pond. This creates even more craziness and can affect every aspect of your life. Not a fun place to be.

So, what can you do to find your path? First, set your intentions according to your passion. Is it a new relationship? A new car? A better job? More money? As simple or complex your wishes are, you can achieve them by taking action. Setting intentions is the first piece of the puzzle. Gauge how you feel like when you ponder what you want. Do you feel that flutter of fear or a flutter of excitement?

I read for a young man who dreamt of being a professional ballroom dancer. He had taken lessons since he was a small child and was now, in his mid-twenties, respected in the industry for his talent and optimism. He loved to teach and inspire others, yet he wasn't following his path. Instead, he worked full time in an office—an office that lacked the creativity that he craved. He said that every morning when he got up, all he saw was black and a piece of him died inside—until he got on the dance floor and something inside of him stirred enough to get by until the next time. When asked why he wasn't teaching or dancing professionally, his response was rife with excuses. A wife who really wanted him to have a "regular job." A father who always wanted him to follow in his footsteps. Two babies to take care of. Now, the babies were a priority, I was with him on that, but as we continued the session, I could tell that while he was trying to please everybody else, he was losing himself. In the end, it would destroy his marriage, his family, and possibly his relationship with his father. We worked out a plan during that forty-five minutes, and I have to say that I held my breath to see if he would email me his family's reaction. Two days later, I received an appointment request from a young lady with the same last name of the dancer and met her the next morning. Instead of being upset with me, she burst into tears of relief. She stated that she could feel the excitement in her husband's voice and the rush of passion not only for the future, but in their relationship—something that had felt blocked for years—and that she wanted help with her life path, too.

Our paths do change over time depending upon responsibilities, but our dreams never should.

Ralph Waldo Emerson said it best when he was quoted as saying, "Always do what you are afraid to do." Sometimes coming out of your comfort zone is enough to get the ball rolling. And if you feel as if you have lost your path, stop and reset your GPS for another destination. This is a journey, not a race, and sometimes when you think you are lost, you may actually have some wonderful experiences.

One day I came home from work stressed and sad. A client was dealing with cancer, and I was helping her overcome some of her fears, but I could see the apprehension in her eyes and her soul as we spoke. The more we talked about the crossing-over process, a man in spirit stepped closer until I could make out his features and could give her full details of who it was. He clearly said "dad." She began to cry as I relayed messages from the person she validated as her father, who had passed away over ten years earlier. He told her that he had been there to help her into the world and would be there just the same to help her on to the Other Side. We both sobbed during the reading, and as we said our goodbyes, I asked her to send me a sign when she was settled in over in heaven.

Now, my dad and I live together and it isn't always the best of times. Not the worst, either, but he is a traditional male. Think Archie Bunker, only not so grumpy. As long as dinner (and it has to be meat and potatoes and dessert) is on the table by five o'clock, life is okay. With my crazy work schedule, that hasn't always been the case, and although my family adjusts fine, he doesn't. I wasn't even in the door when he began to nag me about being hungry and how he wanted dinner. He had also been looking all over for a sponge for the mop and wondered where I put it. I normally walk away quietly, but this time the stress of the day had gotten to me, and I had a temper tantrum—I yelled, screamed, and cried. Instead of Dad reacting with my heightened emotion as he usually does, he grabbed my hand, gave me a hug, and told me that I needed a break. That made me laugh, because it was his nagging that took me to the breaking point. My dad isn't ever quick to say he is sorry, a problem my mom had for years ("Your father always has to be right!"), but I knew that simple hug was his way of apologizing, and I called it good enough.

Often we get caught up in petty arguments and silly grudges. Instead of holding on to all of those emotions (which is the easy thing to do), let go. Release it all because each grudge only holds us back from progressing in life. Think of it as weights in your shoes. Shrug off the weight and walk freely. I was so happy that I did that with my dad.

# thirty-one

# Hope: Full Circle

It had been a horribly long day and I had been at my office for more than eight hours doing readings, conducting radio interviews, and finishing up a writing project. An hour previously I had seen that there was about an inch of snow on top of my car and I moaned. I hated driving in the snow, especially at nighttime. All I wanted was to get home, jump into a hot shower, throw on some flannel PJs and fuzzy socks, and spend some time with my kids before I had to tuck them into bed. Just as I went to shut the final light off, there was a gentle knock on the door. Expecting it to be my landlord or one of my office mates, I was more than surprised to see a young lady standing there. She had mascara-filled tears streaming down her face. Her outfit was a gray sweatshirt, pajama bottoms, and bare feet.

"I...tried...to find you," she said, gasping for air between sobs. "I called where you worked before and they told me you didn't work there, and they didn't know where you were anymore and...I found you."

Turning the lights back on, I gently guided her to the couch and handed her some tissues. It wasn't until after she wiped her eyes that I recognized her. Her name was Hope. Several years back, she and her grandma had come to the shop where I had been reading. She was one of those tough-skinned teenagers who didn't much want to listen to what I had to say, but most of that tough energy was fear. Her mother had been an addict and left her with her grandmother when she was only five years old. When I was reading for her, I had seen badges all over her energy, which to me represented judicial problems. I offered the warning, with more specifics, but she merely shrugged and smirked at me. I had also read for her grandma, Dottie, who had been diagnosed with lung cancer, but didn't much wish to quit smoking or accept the treatment. It didn't take a psychic to see what the end result of that would be.

"She's gone, Kristy," Hope sobbed. "She's gone."

There was an energy that sparkled next to Hope, and I was certain that it was her grandmother. The sparkle, in lieu of an apparition, was my indicator that her grandmother had just passed within the last twenty-four hours. You see, as much as I do see those that have crossed, along with those who are stuck between worlds, the timing is so very important. For the first six months, I tend to only get a sparkle of energy and communication through guides, or what can only be described as telepathy in which I hear the communication in my head. It takes an awful lot of energy for a spirit to manifest into anything larger than that. Those six months (sometimes more) on the Other Side is what I refer to as *Angel Boot Camp*, where they get their orders, choose their housing, reunite with loved ones over there, etc. *And so when scheduling a reading with any medium, it's beneficial to wait at least six months (if not a whole year) after they pass, so that the loved one on the Other Side is strong enough to last an entire session.* They can visit you, but you may not feel them until their energy strengthens. The dream state is often easier for them to come through because you are meeting them in the middle, so to speak. So, there was Hope's grandmother next to her. I could feel that she was concerned, and Hope's spirit guide came through and told me that she was contemplating suicide, thus the pajamas. This wasn't the first time that I had someone show up in pajamas contemplating suicide. One time, the gentleman actually had a gun with him—a danger of my occupation, I suppose. I didn't sense danger with Hope, only grief and guilt. I had felt the exact same with Dottie. Dottie was torn between which world she should be in, wanting so badly to be with her loved ones, but scared to leave Hope. And somehow, someway, Dottie led her to my office.

Hope confessed to me all of the legal trouble she was in after our initial session—the prediction that I saw had come true. Instead of learning the lesson, she instead was angry at the legal system, angry at her mother for abandoning her, and angry at her grandmother for not stopping it. After almost two hours of listening to her and giving her my impressions, I excused myself to attempt to make some late-night phone calls in order to contact those who might help her along her path. After the fourth call, I peeked over to find that Hope had fallen asleep. I called my husband and told him that I would be late, really late. Covering her with a blanket, I turned off most of the lights and closed my eyes. The earlier vision of a hot shower and fuzzy socks became a distant memory and something that didn't seem very important anymore.

Hope woke up several times, sobbing and falling asleep again. Each time, I could feel the pain in Dottie's energy. Her sparkle dimmed. It was several hours later that the young girl woke up. Looking embarrassed, she quickly grabbed her purse to go. I pulled her back to talk about allowing Dottie to leave, allowing her to cross where she could help instead of being stuck. Hope plopped back on the couch and poured her heart out. She spoke of the good and the bad, but a whole lot of ugly, and then she asked Dottie for forgiveness. The light grew brighter around Hope, to the point that she could actually feel the temperature difference. She knew, without me having to explain, that her grandmother was going to be with her no matter what. The light grew dim, little by little, and then it was gone (not as dramatic as *The Ghost Whisperer*, mind you). We both sobbed, as we knew Dottie had crossed.

It was at least a year later, when I was walking through a retail store, that I heard my name called. Turning around,

I saw was a gorgeous young lady, dressed in a business suit and carrying a newborn.

"Kristy, meet Dahlia." The young lady handed me the fair-haired baby girl.

"Your grandmother's favorite flower," I said, tearing up.

Hope nodded and smiled with pride. "I'm working, going to school, in a great relationship, and loving being a mom. I honestly never thought I would get here."

"Amazing what happens when you allow someone to help, huh?" I grinned, referring to her letting her grandma assist her from the Other Side.

I oohed and aahed over the gorgeous baby and then hugged Hope before we said our goodbyes. She finally had found the meaning of her name: Hope.

Oftentimes we get so caught up in our own pride and stubbornness that we forget that not only are there people on this side, but there are people on the Other Side who can help us. We just have to ask.

So, I hope you find some hope in this true story. Whether you are mourning a loved one, going through a financial difficulty, in an unhappy relationship or a job you hate, or whatever, know that all you have to do is ask for assistance. And have hope.

# thirty-two

# *Christmas Socks*

Christmas was a magical time fo me growing up, as it was for most kids, but our household was also filled with a lot of arguing over silly things. Two headstrong parents made it that way.

Every single year, my parents would get into a major argument while decorating the Christmas tree. I can't tell you how many times the tree was thrown out to the curb, ornaments and all, because my dad couldn't get the lights to work. Mom would cry, and I would try to mediate while my brother ran out to gather what he could before the ornaments were stolen. Our next-door neighbor, Aunt Ernie, would yell, asking my parents to stop arguing. I can laugh at the antics now, but back then it was near tragic, or at least I thought it was being all of eight years old.

The holiday season meant time off of school, sledding, family, and new socks. Yes, new socks. Our next-door neighbor, Aunt Ernie, was an ornery redhead who didn't much like women, but put a man in front of her, and she glowed and flirted. Aunt Ernie also pretended that she didn't like kids, yet we could see through her hard façade, especially when she would hand us candy and tell us to hide it, or when she would set up summertime talent shows just to see the neighborhood kids sing and dance. Or when she helped us make lemonade and then became our biggest customer. Aunt Ernie had a heart of gold and a spiked tongue. She worked long hours at the five-and-dime store's cafeteria and let me tell you, she made a dynamite pulled pork sandwich.

Every Christmas Eve, Aunt Ernie would dress in her stained, shiny, faux silk shirt and polyester pants and come over with a pile of gaudy decorated boxes. Each one had a handmade bow and an array of ornaments tied on—none of which anybody would ever think of putting on their tree. The gift inside the box was always the same: socks. As kids, we thought it was the most ridiculous gift ever, but my mom would tell us that one day we would miss them. It sounded like the silliest thing to my sister, brother, and me. Why would we ever miss the annual socks?

When I was twenty years old, I moved out of my childhood home and married my high school sweetheart, during what I truly felt was a magical season: Christmas.

Instead of Aunt Ernie's normal modest attire, the seventy-something aunt by heart showed up at the church in a beautiful emerald velvet gown with a green bow in her auburn hair. She wore the biggest smile on her face, so much that she shined. Her wedding gift to us was—socks.

Aunt Ernie didn't trust the medical community and so when she started to feel ill she ignored it, despite our persistence. Not long after my wedding, Aunt Ernie crossed over to be with Uncle Bill, her husband. It has been years since I thought of that annual gift. Not out of ungratefulness, but I am so emotional that perhaps something so tender to me was best left filed in my memory bank.

There was a time when I felt as if I had strayed off my path. I felt as if I was missing something that I should've been doing and kept seeing angels' wings whenever I meditated. I wasn't so sure what the significance of that was, but I decided to ask for more validation and patiently waited.

And then an elderly lady came in for a reading. Her energy reminded me of my Aunt Ernie, and her husband in spirit who came through reminded me of Uncle Bill. I honestly didn't think she liked her reading. She was very cross with me, and she neither validated nor invalidated anything I had to say; she only scowled. It was a reading that exhausted me because there was no direction.

A few days after the reading, I went into the office on my off day and was retrieving my mail when our mail carrier handed me a small package. He said that a lady had dropped it off, and he wasn't sure how he was going to fit it in my box, so the timing was good.

The box was ornately decorated with a large glittery silver bell. I took it to my office and decided to unwrap it right then and there. Inside was a note that just said "Thank You" from the client I didn't think I had impressed. Underneath the tissue paper was a gift—a pair of socks with angels on them. My Christmas socks. My sign. I picked up my phone to call her with a return *Thank You*, only to get a message that the number was no longer in service.

Everybody comes into our life for a reason and, by paying attention to those who we find along our life journey—even the ornery ones—it only betters our life. Was this client an earth angel or perhaps the spirit of my Aunt Ernie? It could've been both, or neither, but instead of feeling sad about the memory of my annual socks, I was left feeling grateful and thanked Aunt Ernie for coming through with validation.

If you are feeling as if you are missing your path, ask your guides and angels for validation and then trust that they will help lead you back on the path. Maybe things aren't working out because it is part of the path—not the final goal. Stay focused on the outcome and not how you think it will happen. Sometimes the path might not feel right, but it is the final destination that matters most of all. Embrace the fact that you are being guided. Your resistance is what causes the frustration and roadblocks. Let go. Release. Look past the weeds and uncertainty with the knowing that if you simply turn on the Angelic GPS, the way will be discovered.

# thirty-three

# *Heart to Heart*

Sitting down at the small table at the bookstore, I removed my laptop from its carrier and sighed in comfort. I had several pending projects that were pressing and working from home just wasn't cutting it. I could've gone to my office, but that felt like work, and here, well, I could sip a Frappuccino and take in the energy of my favorite thing—books.

I ordered a Caramel Frappuccino (no lectures, please) from the young girl at the counter. She told me that she would bring it out for me. One thing that I have to tell you is that no matter where I go, I can't shut down the spirits. I can try to ignore them, but they are there. Standing next to the barista was a spirit that looked like the girl's grandfather. He stood tall, with gray hair and mischievous green eyes. His spirit felt fresh, as if he had just recently crossed over, and he had a worried look on his face. I smiled at him, he smiled back (yes, they know when I am there, too!), and I sat back down at my table. I had just started to type out something witty, or at least I so, when the girl came over with my drink. Her mood was melancholy, but she was doing a very good job pretending to be all right.

"Are you okay?" I asked her.

She forced a smile and nodded, tears filling her eyes.

"Want to talk about it?"

She shook her head. "I'm probably just sleep deprived. Or hormonal," she said, laughing. Moving to the table next to me, she started to clean.

I looked over at her grandfather, who gestured for me to keep talking to her. A pushy man, I thought. I rarely intervene, but I didn't feel like being haunted by anybody after I left, so I thought it best to get this done with now.

"Well, you might think that I'm the one sleep deprived. Or crazy," I said, grabbing her attention again. "But, did you just lose your grandpa?"

That obviously got her attention and she simply stared at me with wide eyes.

"Ye … yes. How did … ?"

"It's sort of my thing," I replied, waving my hand like it wasn't anything big. "He's standing next to you and looks quite worried."

Looking beside her, and obviously seeing nothing, she eyed me curiously. "He died a few days ago, and every single night since then I've been having dreams." She hesitated a moment. "Well, not even dreams. It's hard to explain."

"Visits," I said. "They're visits, not dreams. He stands next to you and is talking to you, right? And you can remember every single piece of information right down to the clothes you both are wearing."

"Yes!" she said, looking amazed.

"They aren't dreams because he truly is standing right next to you, and he really is trying to get through to you." I looked over at her grandpa to get some information and continued. "He says that he had been trying to have a heart to heart with you for a while, but you were too busy."

Her face crumbled and tears began to fall. "I didn't even go to the hospital."

"Please, he doesn't want you to feel guilty or sad. That isn't the point of his message. He wants you to know that you will be the best preschool teacher ever, but you need to start setting priorities." I sighed before I continued, but Mr. Antsy Pants was making sure all information was given. "He isn't fond of your boyfriend, and he says that he knows that he talks down to you and is emotionally abusive. That is the reason you've been avoiding your family. You're afraid to hear the truth. He wants you to take control of your life again and know that he will be there for you as you find your identity." I looked at her grandpa to make sure I didn't forget anything. "Oh, and he loves you and is happy that you have the key."

The girl swallowed hard. She pulled out a necklace that was tucked under her shirt and showed me a small charm…of a key. "He gave this to me when I was about ten years old. I put it on the day of his funeral. The dreams ... visits ... started that same night."

"Listen to what he has to say. Keep a notepad by your bed and write down the information. Our loved ones on the Other Side are there to help; we just have to ask them for the guidance and assistance. The heart-to-hearts don't have to end when the physical body leaves."

She offered me a hug and, shaking her head in disbelief, walked back to the counter. And I sat down to write.

My clients come to me to help validate that their loved ones are okay on the Other Side. You don't need me or any other medium; you simply need to learn how to shut out the static of this world to listen to your angels, guides, and loved ones. When we panic or feel as if the world has turned on us—when we need advice and healing the most—the white noise becomes even louder. Ironic. The reason for this is vibrations. When we panic, we lower our vibration, which puts us out of sync with the vibration that we need. By cleaning the negative filter, you can rise to a higher vibration, which can help push the messages through clearer. Think of it like this: When you panic or get frustrated, the windows around you begin to fog. You can attempt to wipe them, but they will continue to fog unless you utilize a tool (a defrost button) to unfog so that the light can shine in with clear messages. Tools can include meditation, writing/journaling, exercise, massage, talking with a friend (not complaining, but talking), or taking a bath or shower. Or maybe even sipping a Frappuccino.

# thirty-four

# *With Love*

Very often I have clients in my office who ache that they weren't able to say that last "I love you," or feel that the person they lost might not have known how they felt. Sometimes the littlest thing in life changes something forever. Don't live with regrets. Live with love.

He was dying and she wasn't quite sure what she would do without him. The heart surgery was do or die, but the surgeon had already warned that the chances of survival weren't good. All they could do was hope for a miracle and go through with the surgery.

Nick and Betty married when they were just eighteen years old and soon after had two sons they both doted on. Except for Betty staying in the hospital after having the boys, they had never been apart, so leaving Nick in the hospital, fighting for his life for the past week, had been absolute torture for Betty. She asked if she could sleep in the chair next to him, but the nurses reassured her that he was well taken care of and that she needed rest, too. Reluctantly, she would go home, pet their Maltese, Patches, and sob herself to sleep, praying that God would give her the strength and give Nick the strength to survive.

February 14 was, ironically, the date of Nick's surgery. It also was their wedding anniversary. She tried to believe it was an omen of good luck. After all, heart surgery on Valentine's Day had to mean something. Or so Betty tried to convince herself. She said her goodbyes to him as they wheeled him into surgery, her bright blue eyes sparkling with tears.

"XOXO," he said to her, smiling and giving her the thumbs-up.

Betty laughed. Nick rarely said "I love you," but instead would say "XOXO." She gave him a final kiss and watched until the large white double doors closed and he was out of sight. Her sons, one on each side of her, led her to the waiting room. They had been forewarned that if he survived, the recovery would be long and it would probably be a few days before he was cognitive. Betty didn't care. She would wait; he was worth it. She loved his tousled gray hair and his sparkling green eyes. She loved his five o'clock shadow and the way that he left his coffee cup on the table, always making stains. She loved the way he smelled after his walks Up North and how he would nuzzle into her neck, keeping her awake with his soft snores. Sure, they fought, but the good always outweighed the bad. She could never understand the pettiness she saw on talk shows, or even what she heard from her co-workers at the office. If you love, you love forever and you love no matter what. Or as Nick would say—XOXO. She couldn't wait to hear Nick give her that thumbs-up and tell her, only the way that he could, how he loved her. XOXO.

Betty didn't want to upset the kids or grandkids, so she kept taking deep breaths, pushing the sobs away, and just stared at her book, never turning a page.

It had been three hours since Nick was taken back and the doctor came in for an update.

His words sounded muffled as he told the family that it didn't look promising and they were doing everything that they could, but to expect the worse. Several hours later when Betty held Nick's hand, trying to avoid the many tubes and wires, she knew. Even though he was technically alive, she didn't feel his spirit. He was gone. The clock ticked to 12:01 a.m., February 15, and Nick took his last breath. She knew that he'd waited to cross so that their wedding anniversary wouldn't be thought of as his death date.

Betty functioned only by keeping busy with funeral arrangements and consoling her family and friends. After all, it was how Betty was. But the night after Nick was laid to rest, she sat down at the kitchen table where they had shared years of laughs, tears, and worries along with pounds of coffee, and she laid her head down and asked God to take her too, and if He wouldn't to at least give her a sign that there was an afterlife. She was doubting. Even though it was Nick's heart that gave out, it was hers that hurt.

A basket of sympathy cards was in front of her and she thought perhaps if she began to go through those and write out her thanks to those who attended the funeral, she could keep her mind occupied. Several cards in, she noticed one that had familiar writing on it. She mostly saw it on grocery lists and not on cards, but she took the letter opener and gently opened it. The card was an anniversary card from Nick.

*Dear Betty,*
*You know that I never have been one for words, but even though I am away from you, I had to let you know...*
*XOXO,*
*Nick*

We receive letters from Heaven each day. It might not be in the form of a piece of paper or a note card, but if you just listen you might hear that XOXO.

# thirty-five

## *Sally*

A brisk Friday in the spring of 2008, I opened my office door to greet my next client. Her name was Sally, and she offered a bright smile as I gestured for her to sit down on the brown wicker couch. Sally was dressed in jeans and a white T-shirt adorned with embroidered butterflies. On her head, she wore a fuchsia bandana. It didn't take a psychic to know that she was battling cancer.

I have always had a difficult time reading for those with cancer—it physically stings me to look at those stricken. I have been a psychic medium since my first memory at three years old and have been around death several times over, but when I looked at Sally—well, something was different.

"Did you want a general reading?" I asked, already knowing what her reply would be.

"No, Kristy, what I want is for you to tell me what heaven is like." Sally's blue eyes brightened as tears ran down her cheek.

I pulled my chair closer to her and took her hands in mine, offering as much comfort as I could give.

"I know that I am dying and I know that it is soon," Sally sniffled and then raised her shoulders in pride. "I don't want to know when..."

"Good, because I won't tell death dates," I said.

I wrapped us both in the blue light of healing and began.

The reading ran well over our allotted time, and I was very grateful she was my last appointment. During that hour plus, I brought in her husband and other family members. I knew that her end was mere days away as those on the Other Side gathered in waiting. We discussed the pets that she would reunite with and laughed about how she would be able to nag her husband again. We cried, laughed, and cried more. Sally's sense of humor remained intact and I was truly awed at her courage.

When I walked her to the office building's front door, she grabbed me in a hug and thanked me.

"I will let you know when I get to the Other Side," Sally promised.

"Please do," I responded with a smile. I shoved my hands in my sweater pocket and pulled out a rose quartz stone. I didn't know when or how it even got there, but I took that as a sign and handed it to her. "For your trip."

She took the stone, rubbed it lovingly with her thumb and index finger, placed it in her purse, and left.

My weekend was filled with the normal chaos that a family of four kids, a husband, and five dogs bring about, not to mention a calendar of clients. It wasn't that I didn't think of Sally, but I didn't want to dwell on her end, which truly was her new beginning. Sally had two children and five grandchildren, and I knew what they would be going through, as I had lost my own mom two years before. Sally and my mom shared one thing—they had the same name. But even with being a psychic medium and being very grateful for the gift, I was very sensitive to the sadness that went along with it.

Tuesday afternoon I ran out to our mailbox; bill, bill, advertisement, card…The return address simply stated "*Heaven*" and I smiled as I opened it.

> *Kristy,*
>
> *I just wanted to thank you again for giving me peace during my transition. I will be sure to tell your mom that you said hello and give her a hug from you.*
>
> *Love,*
> *Sally*

Something pulled me to open the obituaries, and sure enough, Sally's picture smiled back at me. Her crossing over date was noted as Monday, three days after our appointment.

Well over a week after Sally's passing I ventured out to the mall to do some window-shopping. As I was browsing at the trinkets, a lady who looked to be in her mid-thirties came up to me.

"Excuse me," she said, nervously pulling back her shoulder-length brown hair.

I looked at her, puzzled.

"This may seem crazy," she said.

"Try me," I urged, curiously.

Reaching into her pocket, she pulled out a stone and handed it to me. "Something tells me you had to have this. I don't know why, but I couldn't leave the store without doing this."

Taking the stone from her, I grinned to see that it was a rose quartz. Not the same one that I gave Sally, but a rose quartz just the same.

"Not crazy at all," I replied in awe. "Thank you."

"No, thank YOU. I was hoping you weren't going to think I was nuts!" The lady laughed and walked away without allowing me to give her validation.

What I have discovered in life is that there's no such thing as a coincidence, only universal synchronicity. I don't believe that it was a coincidence that my client and my mom shared the same name, and I don't believe that it was a coincidence that a complete stranger walked up to me in a public location and handed me the same kind of stone that I had given Sally. Oftentimes we get so caught up in the drama of the outside world that we become blind to the signs all around us. Whether a penny you pick up at the gas station or a feather you "mysteriously" find on your car seat—your angels and loved ones from the other side are continually showing you their love.

My mom didn't know that I worked as a psychic medium until just a few weeks before her death, and this occurrence made me feel as if she accepted me for who I am.

As I stroked my new stone, I knew that my mom and my client were hugging and Mom was showing her around the place.

# thirty-six

# Haunting the Haunted

My entire life has revolved around the paranormal. If it didn't find me, I sought it. Lunch hours were frequently taken at the local historical cemetery where I would have peaceful conversations with those crossed over, and ghosts-in-waiting. Not once during my excursions did I stomp and storm about, forcing them to show themselves, or demand them to make lights flicker on my meters, or enforce that they move a toy. Well, it did (and still does) help that I am a medium and can see, sense, hear, and communicate with those on the Other Side of life. But just like many other people, I have watched my fair share of paranormal shows. Some I love, some I tolerate, and then there are some that I just shake my head at in total disgust. If you have attended any of the ghost tours, ghost hunts, or overnights that I have hosted, you know that the first thing I say is that ghost hunting is as exciting as watching paint dry. And the next thing that I say is to respect the spirits and ghosts. We live as one, under a different sky, a different paradigm, but still as one. So yelling and screaming in their home, or at them, and requesting that they do circus tricks...well, it just doesn't cut it. It is disrespectful. Even snapping zillions of photographs, as if you are the paranormal paparazzi, is ridiculous.

Over the past few years, I have found so-called haunted locations noting on their contracts that it will not be allowed for anyone in a group to cross-over a spirit. *That they like their ghosts.* I wonder if they would feel the same way if the tables were turned and they missed the last train to heaven. How they would feel being kept hostage? It is wise to think of paranormal situations as if the person is standing in front of you. Would you tell that person, "Sorry, I like the money that I am making off of you, therefore you aren't allowed to leave to be with your family?" Although I have come into contact with some soulless people in my lifetime, I doubt that many would have the guts to say that. So just because you cannot see these beings, why do so many feel that they have a stake in keeping them hostage? They don't, and shouldn't, and for those who do, just know that there may be a lovely karmic situation for you when you pass.

So is ghost hunting entertainment or really something more serious? In 2012 I took a group of ghost seekers to the old historic Jackson Prison (1837–1935) in Jackson, Michigan, that is now called Armory Arts Village. What once held inmates in four tiers of prison cells is now a beautiful artist community with apartments, condominiums, and art studios. But kept intact are solitary confinement cells and the old tunnels where unimaginable things happened to the prisoners, for it was "out of sight." I am cautious where I take the public, as I have gone toe-to-toe with a demon and survived (obviously), but it is nothing that I would ever recommend to a novice or even an expert investigator. I didn't feel awful about Michigan's first state prison. It felt like a safe place, and I was assured by tenants that although there is so much activity, it has never been negative.

The night wasn't too eventful until Jackson lost power after a drunken driver ran into a transformer. Most of the group left after that (whether tired or scared...we may never know), and we were left with a core group of investigators interested in venturing down into the tunnel once more. As we sat crouched and waiting, we all began to feel as if we were the ones hunted. The energy shifted into something that felt almost mocking. With our instruments lighting up, and a toy car being moved with ethereal hands, we heard whispers. To break up the tension, we decided on a sing-along, which entertained both the group and the ghosts. At one point, we received a message from a man who wanted to cross over. He was done being stuck. He was done hiding from his judgment, for possibly he had already served it and knew it. So I did what any good investigator should do—I asked the group to help me cross him over. The energy shifted; it lifted. Many in the group sniffled. I cried. I didn't cry because I was afraid that the next group that I brought in might be ghostless; I cried because we'd helped reunite this spirit with his family and friends after so much time. He may have never received that opportunity if it wasn't for us. Not once did I think of just walking away from him. Call me a sucker, or a helper, or even a healer; I would refer to the whole group as ghost Samaritans. And maybe that is why the power went out. And maybe that is why we decided to venture down there instead of someone's apartment, which was on the itinerary. There is nothing random in life; there is always a reason.

When we left, I didn't feel as if I had given the group an entertaining time. I think some may have left thinking back to the beginning of the lecture and agreeing that ghost hunting was indeed much like watching paint dry and they would probably never do it again, while I think others felt the adrenaline of helping, not just hunting.

So next time you watch one of the paranormal shows, look to see if the teams are mocking, hunting, hurting, or healing the field. It will indeed open your eyes to the Other Side.

# thirty-seven

# Remember Me

"I'm afraid I've been forgotten."

It was 2:45 a.m. and I'd been awoken by the dead. I was startled to open my eyes and see the lost spirit of a man in his sixties with beautiful blue eyes and dark brown hair standing next to my bed. I moaned and then felt guilty. For the past two weeks I hadn't slept. My bedroom had been a revolving door for the dead, which meant that I was exhausted in body, mind, and spirit. I was tempted to put a "Do Not Disturb—that means even the dead" sign on my door, but had a feeling that they wouldn't listen. Heck, the living didn't seem to care whether I was busy or tired and needed rest, why would spirits care?

I grabbed my cell phone to help light my way to the family room, trying not to trip over the obstacle course of animals on the floor. The pets were all so used to the chaos in the home, and ghosts or spirits just didn't seem to startle them much; it didn't comfort me any to think that would their response be the same if a criminal broke in.

"Now what's your problem?" I whispered.

"I'm afraid I've been forgotten," the man repeated.

"Who do you think has forgotten you?" My tone rose slightly. It was almost 3 a.m. now and I was in no mood to play charades or guessing games.

"My wife. She's stopped talking to me. She doesn't visit my grave and I've only been gone ... " He thought for a moment. "Maybe two years."

Time doesn't mean much to the Other Side, like it does to us, so I wasn't surprised that he wasn't sure how long it had been since he'd passed on. If you ever watch paranormal shows, you might see investigators asking the spirits if they know what year it is or to tell them what year they think it is.

"Do you visit her, though ... ?"

"Pete. My name's Pete. Yes, I sit by her at night and I watch her cry, but I can't help her. I don't want to see her cry, but I don't want her to forget the good times that we had. We did have good times. I don't want her to forget who I was, but I'm afraid she's only remembering the sickness, the sadness. How do I help?"

Now normally I am visited by those who need help to cross over, or those confused and lost. Sometimes I have spirits who ask me to give a message to their loved one, but I will not be an ambulance chaser and search out their loved ones like the character in the show *Ghost Whisperer*. Pete's predicament was different, though. He was actually looking for a counseling session himself.

"You help by showing her the happiness again. Give her a happy sign. The sadness won't go away, but it will fade, and maybe if you show her something that made her happy, she will smile and not cry. It takes time, Pete. You may be in paradise, but those living still have to deal and cope with the loss."

Pete nodded.

"And by the way, why are you upset she doesn't go to your grave? You aren't there," I asked curiously.

"Yes, but I get all of her attention when she is there." His eyes flashed for a moment and he continued. "But I'm sure that it just makes her sad to visit."

"So you know what to do, right?"

"I was an engineer, Kristy. I was never good with romance when it came to being alive, and now I have to romance her while being dead? Women..."

"Night, Pete."

Every single day there is tragedy, and every minute of the day someone loses someone who is their world and their reality has to change. Those who die aren't lost, even though it may feel like that as we mourn the loss. In your mourning, though, don't forget to remember the good times and know that they are trying to comfort and give you signs that make you smile. Love doesn't die; it continues to live on through the soul and the spirit.

# thirty-eight

# *Blooming*

Her name was Allison. The apprehensive way she approached my office door made it clear she had never sought a consultation of this kind before. I greeted her with a smile and a hug and led her to the couch to chat for a bit. She didn't make an appointment to connect with anybody on the Other Side or to hear what her future might hold, but instead she needed some life coaching. Or at least that is what she had ordered.

Allison, a pretty lady with long, light brown strands that she held messily on top of her head with a large purple clip, went on to explain what she wanted out of her life situation. As I always do, no matter the service you sign up for, I was checking in with the Other Side to see and hear the truths behind the lines. She told me that she had recently lost her job in the accounting field and that her dream was to open a bakery. Although she was often told she was a great baker, she didn't know how to do it on a large scale and had never run a business. She needed money. She needed investments and hadn't a clue where to start. It had her so stressed out that she was going to leave my office and start submitting applications to Target and J.C. Penney because she was so afraid that her unemployment wasn't going to pay the bills, pay for Christmas, and … on and on and on. The pressure cooker of her life created scattered energy. You could see it in her face, hear it in her voice, and I could see her guide's frustration because her fear of the future was helping to create exactly what she didn't want. She didn't want to work at Target or J.C. Penney. She didn't want to be broke. She didn't want to be unhappy. But she was heading straight down that path. Now you might be saying, "But Kristy, you sometimes have to do things that you don't want to and she has to have money!" Yes, that is true, but…

What happened next was like a scene from a movie. A lady who looked much like Allison, only forty years older, came forward from the Other Side to connect. She smiled at me, tears streaming down her face with the love that she felt when she looked at her daughter, but also sadness because Allison couldn't see or hear her.

"Allison, your mom has crossed, right? I have her here and she wants to talk."

Allison looked at me as if I had just told her aliens had landed and they were going to take her away for a bit. But then the message sunk in and she began to sob. She shook her head for me to continue.

"Please tell her that I have always believed in her, but it is my fault that she even went into accounting to begin with. I wanted something stable and steady for her. She was always in her element in the kitchen. Hair mussed, creating..."

The message was passed along, and Allison laughed.

"It's true. She didn't want me to ever have to rely on a man for an income. After my father left us with absolutely nothing when I was eight years old, she learned real quick what being independent meant and she taught me that steady and stable wins the race. Now, isn't that funny that in this economy that isn't necessarily so?"

Her mom sat down next to her and the breeze of the energy change moved a picture on the wall that was painted with the words "Believe." Allison quickly turned around at the noise and then looked back at me for an explanation.

"She's sitting next to you and wanted to get your attention."

"She always used to tell me that she believed in me. I forgot about that. It has been a long time since someone believed in me."

I smiled, tears forming in my eyes. "Ready to get to work?"

Allison's energy brightened and she happily nodded. You could feel the fear from just minutes before begin to evaporate as she realized that she had cheerleaders.

I won't go into details of her business plan, but I will tell you that although she hasn't (yet) opened her bakery, she is not working at Target or J.C. Penney. Instead, she is now in the field she so longed to be in, learning how to run a business. She has an investor interested in her ideas and her accounting background did indeed help her, since as part of the business she has to project numbers for inventory. Mom knew what she was doing, after all.

I rarely treat myself to fun. A sad truth. But I hadn't been feeling well, was exhausted and energy depleted, and decided that not only me, but also the family, deserved to have some forced family fun time. And so on a Saturday we set off for lunch and then to see the movie *Tangled*. Now, call me silly, but I even cry at cartoons. There is a moment near the middle to end of the movie where Rapunzel was sitting in a boat with Flynn awaiting the release of the lanterns, something that she wanted so badly to see, when fear took hold and she began to worry that she might be disappointed that it wouldn't live up to her high expectations. She asked what she would do then and how would she cope. Flynn told her that no matter what happened, she would go on to find a new dream.

When we experience fear or frustration, we immediately tense up our body, mind, and spirit, which hinders the flow of what we do want to come to us, and we begin to visualize everything that we DON'T want instead of what we DO. So, if you are experiencing frustration (or fear) with any aspect of your life—career, money, love, etc—take a few moments a day visualizing how you want that area to look. When you begin to say negative things like, "I will never have money to do the things I want," say "Stop" and then repeat what you do want—"I have enough money to do the things that I want." It takes some training, but before you know it, the things you don't want will begin to stop happening and the things that you do want will start flowing. Now, we are always tested, so be on guard so that you can pass the test. And know, always know, that there are those who believe in you and that with every dream accomplished, or even a dream failed, remember that the most important thing is for you to continually dream the dream. No matter what.

I recall going through one of my several tough patches and falling asleep crying in my pillow and waking up feeling lost. It wasn't until I allowed myself to see through the fog of life that I realized that I was keeping that fog around me—nobody else was. It was a hard lesson for me to learn, that I was essentially causing the stagnant pain around me instead of dreaming of new possibilities. My thoughts throughout the day (and the afternoon and the night) were essentially everything that I didn't want in my life, and yet I was the one feeding it and helping it grow.

If you don't want weeds to grow in your garden, you pull them, you don't feed them, right? And yet, that is exactly what we do every single day. You want a love life? Then don't focus on not having a love life. You want financial freedom? Then don't focus on not having any money. You want a new job? Then stop focusing on how much you hate your job and start looking for a new one! If you continue to live in the same way, day after day after day, you are sure to get depressed and sad, so create a new day with new thoughts. Every night before bed, ask yourself what you want the next day to be like. Every morning, as soon as you awake, become aware of every thought that you think because your thoughts help to construct your reality.

Several years back, I woke up one day and thought—if I could create a superhero identity for myself, what would it entail? I grabbed a notebook and began to construct the person who I wanted to be, not who I was. I didn't add flying or invisibility to my list, but I thought big and I thought larger than life and I began little by little to construct that Super Hero. Instead of going to bed thinking how awful my life was, I would write in my gratitude journal (even if I wasn't feel very grateful) and the first thing I did when I awoke was to add a list of goals to my day because that way I was keeping my thoughts away from what I didn't want. I can't say that it was easy at first, but if I can do it, anyone can! You can't move forward if you are still haunted by the past, even if you think that you have patched it up and sunk it deep away. If you haven't released it, it still impacts you in some ways, and by weeding your garden and planting new thoughts in your day, you will be amazed at the blossoms that will appear.

## thirty-nine

# *Letting Love In*

Valentine's Day may be just another day to some, but to others it is special. Even though we are supposed to express our love to one another each and every day, February 14 is an opportunity for those who can't easily communicate it. My parents were married on Valentine's Day, and my mom would always say, "Don't ever get married on Valentine's Day because you won't get an anniversary gift or a Valentine's Day gift." That typically wasn't true, but in her mind it was. I always had a hopeless romantic notion of Valentine's Day and not one of my husbands (including Chuck) are very romantic in the sense of gift giving. Over time, I learned that I would much rather have a meaningful hug and kiss than a gift. Or maybe I just tell myself that.

Right before Valentine's Day, I was perusing the seasonal aisle at a local store. A little boy gently took the Valentine's

Day packets down from the shelf, one by one. He would hold each one for a second, shake his head, put it back, and take another down and repeat. I was curious as to what he was doing, so in a non-stalker, non-threatening way, I looked through the candy on the other side of the aisle. About three minutes later, I heard a small voice behind me say, "Excuse me." I turned to see the brown-haired boy with large green eyes standing next to me, looking crestfallen.

"Yes?" I asked him, now even more curious. I always seemed to be a magnet to kids and cats, which was just fine with me.

"Can you help me choose a Valentine for my mom?"

I looked around to see who he was with. As if reading my mind, he pointed across the aisle.

"My dad is over there and my mom and dad have been fighting lately. He said he wasn't going to get her anything for Valentine's Day, so I thought that maybe if I did, they'd stop fighting. I have $5." He smiled and held up his bill.

I cannot tell you how badly I wanted to cry right then, but I held it together and walked with him to the card section. The cards he was looking at weren't for adults—they were boxes of cartoon characters that you would give out to a class, but I didn't want to criticize.

"Well, what was the one that you first thought she would like, the first one you picked up?"

He thought for a second and walked over to a pink packet that had kittens on it. "These," he proclaimed proudly.

"Then I think that those will do the job perfectly." I smiled, wanting so badly to give him a hug.

"Thank you. I think so, too. Mom loves kittens." He held the packet close to him.

"Have a great Valentine's Day, and give your mom a hug from me."

He nodded, still looking at his cards, and joined his dad. That little boy had the weight of the world on his shoulders, unbeknownst to his parents, and he was going to use the Hallmark holiday to proclaim his love to his mom and attempt to heal his parents' marriage.

As you and I both know, that young boy can't save a marriage, but as I mentioned I am a hopeless romantic and I hope that they saw the hurt they were causing and tried to make amends. Releasing the bitterness and anger against someone you love (or once loved) is more healing than burying it. The more the anger piles up, the more the heart gets weighed down with negativity. We then fall off our soul path.

When people we love hurt us, it is a natural reaction to want to shield ourselves and put protection around our hearts, to keep the pain from entering. A shut-down heart makes it impossible to open up and allow in happiness, great opportunities, and good people. However, when you open your heart, you have room for growth, forgiveness, and change. Most of all, you can let love in, again.

*Epilogue*

## Dream Chasers

I don't believe that I live an extraordinary life, but instead treat each moment of my life as extraordinary. I take in the world around me, and by doing so, I find that extraordinary opportunities surround me. When people call me special or gifted, I admit that I shudder. The expectations of such statements seem much too high of a standard to live up to. I would rather be called "in tune," as I am merely an instrument, a messenger from the Other Side to this side. I have always strived to be normal, although I live a life anything but.

I have done my share of press and media blitzes, most of which ask me the same thing over and over. "How do you do readings?" It sounds like such a simple question, but the explanation is really quite complex. When I read for someone for the first time, I have my spiel of explaining that I talk to angels, along with guides, both the client's and my own, who give me information that I then pass along to them. I also talk to those who have crossed over and they also pass along pertinent information that can be validated—sometimes immediately and other times not until the client rids herself/himself of psychic amnesia (that is when the client either gets nervous or blanks out). I am the medium between this world and the other. A bridge, if you will, that helps connect. Sometimes I hear things. Other times I see the spirit. Sometimes I get names. Other times I only get a feeling of energy. I see things in my mind's eye or get visions that play like a movie. A lot of times they, the loved one or guide, stands right in front of me as clear as day. Sometimes the spirit is talkative and will give me a ton of information that the client can relate to and other times the spirit is quiet and plays hard to get. No reading is ever the cookie-cutter kind.

I was born a people pleaser. I want everybody around me to be happy, which includes my clients. Obviously that is impossible, but I still strive to give my very best. Sometimes, though, when I do readings, what the guides are telling me is not as warm and fuzzy and positive as I would like. There are times that I have to tell people what they don't want to hear. And, every time that happens, it truly breaks my heart. I learned early on, however, that it does no good to tell people what they want to hear instead of what they need to hear. Some may feel that I am not connecting to them, but let me know in six months to a year if that is true or if it is really just tunnel vision. I have to say, however, that those types of readings honestly upset me to the point that I second-guess myself, and second-guess the guides (which they don't like so well). I want Happily Ever After for everyone, which is a fault of mine. I want to help my clients attain the path to exactly that because I don't believe it is a faraway land.

We all have free will. One of my favorite quotes hangs in my office: "Destiny is not a matter of chance, but a matter of choice." We all have a choice to either go on this path or go on that path over there. Or maybe even that one *way* over there. The point is that our hands are never tied. Some paths are much more difficult to get to, just as Robert Frost writes in "The Road Not Taken." In my life I choose to blaze my own path, albeit it took me a while to get to that path, and because of that I am not always the fan favorite. I tried the more conservative path of school, corporate life, and the nine-to-five day... it isn't that I can't do it; I don't care to do it. Lazy has never been a word that ever described me. I am continually chopping down my path each moment that I can. You may not physically see the headway that I am making, but it is there. I admit, some days I am more ambitious than others... hey, I'm human... but action of some sort has to be done in order to continue with growth! You will rarely, if ever, come to me for a reading and hear me say that what I "see" is what you will get no matter what. I describe what is down each path for you, be it the one on the left or the one on the right or the one right in front of you. Our lives are not carved in stone. Your future is continuously unfolding with each action that you take right now.

One day when I was talking to my husband about the way I do readings, he explained it best: "Kristy, you are just the piano player, not the songwriter." How true that is. You are the songwriter of your life; I only tell you what your guides show me. If you don't like the song that I'm playing (or that another medium or psychic is playing), start writing a new song.

You hear of people chasing their dreams; well, if you truly want your dreams to become a reality, you have to get wet once in a while. Take a chance. Don't run. Fear of not receiving the desired outcome will get you exactly that—nothing.

There are times when I know that I am trying too hard and that trying results in chasing. Chasing and taking action are two different things in my book, and the best way to determine which is which is by your emotion. Chasing results is that feeling you get when you jog around the block—heart palpitating, sweaty, and out of breath—while action feels confident and you don't have to get the deodorant out for another round.

I have had my share of roadblocks, but those roadblocks are there for a reason. Those who truly are passionate about their path will find a detour to get to it, or just plow straight through. A way will be found. Others who find roadblocks in their path of vision will give up, and maybe that is a good thing, because if they don't have the passion to find a way to the other side of that wall, they really don't belong there. Without passion, you are left with only emptiness.

I named my company *Tangled Wishes* because so many have dreams and aspirations, but they are often tangled up, much like a mess of Christmas tree lights. Sometimes it takes Soul Work, patience, and believing again in yourself to rediscover that light within and unpack your dreams from storage. And, just like with Christmas lights, you have to plug them in to see if they work and maybe even make adjustments.

Even if we have never met, or never will, know that I believe in you. Now go unpack and create your Happily-After-After.

# GET MORE AT **LLEWELLYN.COM**

Visit us online to browse hundreds of our books and decks, plus sign up to receive our e-newsletters and exclusive online offers.

- **Free tarot readings • Spell-a-Day • Moon phases**
- **Recipes, spells, and tips • Blogs • Encyclopedia**
- **Author interviews, articles, and upcoming events**

# GET SOCIAL WITH **LLEWELLYN**

### Find us on Facebook

www.Facebook.com/LlewellynBooks

Follow us on

www.Twitter.com/Llewellynbooks

# GET BOOKS AT **LLEWELLYN**

## LLEWELLYN ORDERING INFORMATION

**Order online:** Visit our website at www.llewellyn.com to select your books and place an order on our secure server.

**Order by phone:**
- Call toll free within the U.S. at 1-877-NEW-WRLD (1-877-639-9753)
- Call toll free within Canada at 1-866-NEW-WRLD (1-866-639-9753)
- We accept VISA, MasterCard, and American Express

**Order by mail:**
Send the full price of your order (MN residents add 6.875% sales tax) in U.S. funds, plus postage and handling to: Llewellyn Worldwide, 2143 Wooddale Drive, Woodbury, MN 55125-2989

**POSTAGE AND HANDLING:**

STANDARD: (U.S. & Canada)
(Please allow 2 business days)
$25.00 and under, add $4.00.
$25.01 and over, FREE SHIPPING.

INTERNATIONAL ORDERS (airmail only):
$16.00 for one book, plus $3.00 for each additional book.

Visit us online for more shipping options. Prices subject to change.

### *FREE CATALOG!*

To order, call
1-877-
NEW-WRLD
ext. 8236
or visit our
website

BARBARA PARKS

in the presence of

spirits

a true story of ghostly visitations

# In the Presence of Spirits
## *A True Story of Ghostly Visitations*
### Barbara Parks

Traumatized by vicious poltergeist attacks that lasted five years, Barbara Parks never imagined that her deep-rooted fear of ghosts would disappear. A momentous turning point occurs when, still mourning the sudden death of a beloved friend, she receives a miraculous visit from him. This joyous experience marks her first step toward healing—and opening up to the spirit world.

*In the Presence of Spirits* chronicles Barbara's uplifting, personal journey of gradually accepting and embracing the clairvoyant gifts that allow her to see spirits. She shares dramatic and heartwarming stories of interacting with spirits who turn up everywhere: at home, on vacation, and accompanying her patients. From the departed uncle that protects Barbara's young children from grave injury to the child spirits who bring comfort to their parents, these amazing true tales are convincing reminders that our loved ones are never far away.

**978-0-7387-3352-4, 240 pp., 5³⁄₁₆ x 8**         **$15.99**

---